Amy

LIGHT
THE WAY

A Guide to Becoming a Rescue Medium

REDFeather
MIND | BODY | SPIRIT

Library of Congress Control Number: 2017954757

Designed by Brenda McCallum
Cover design by Brenda McCallum
Type set in Zurich/Times

ISBN: 978-0-7643-5508-0
Printed in China

Published by Red Feather Mind, Body, Spirit
An imprint of Schiffer Publishing, Ltd.
4880 Lower Valley Road
Atglen, PA 19310
Phone: (610) 593-1777; Fax: (610) 593-2002
E-mail: Info@schifferbooks.com
Web: www.redfeatherpub.com

For our complete selection of fine books on this and related subjects, please visit our website at www.schifferbooks.com. You may also write for a free catalog.

Schiffer Publishing's titles are available at special discounts for bulk purchases for sales promotions or premiums. Special editions, including personalized covers, corporate imprints, and excerpts, can be created in large quantities for special needs. For more information, contact the publisher.

We are always looking for people to write books on new and related subjects. If you have an idea for a book, please contact us at proposals@schifferbooks.com.

Other Schiffer Books on Related Subjects:

The Reluctant Empath. Bety Comerford and Steve Wilson
ISBN: 978-0-7643-4603-3

The Empath's Quest: Finding Your Destiny. Bety Comerford and Steve Wilson
ISBN: 978-0-7643-5223-2

The Empathic Ghost Hunter. Bety Comerford and Steve Wilson
ISBN: 978-0-7643-5409-0

Joseph Durmaa (signature)

CONTENTS

Preface

Welcome to the world of spirit rescue. In this book, you will find information and guidance on how to become a rescue medium. In no way is this book meant to replace training by a specialized rescue medium. Rather, it is meant to supplement your training by providing the knowledge that will help you on your journey.

Like many other rescue mediums, I didn't have a mentor to question or book to consult. Most of the information I've learned came from my spiritual teachers, observing other mediums in the field, trial and error, and listening to the earthbound spirits themselves. Like life itself, my education was a process of discovery. Every experience I encountered helped me gain more of an understanding of the world of the earthbound spirit and my role in their healing and transition.

Light the Way is intended to guide you through the necessary steps needed to train in the field of spirit rescue. Topics will include:

- Rescue mediumship techniques
- Understanding your spiritual team
- Telling the difference between spirits by their vibration
- Psychic and spiritual protection
- Common tools of the trade
- Prayers and affirmations
- Ways to help you improve your connection to spirit

In my first book, *Toward the Light*, I briefly explained the role of a rescue medium and suggested a few methods to start developing the skill set. I stated that everyone has the ability to connect with spirit energy and communicate in their own unique way. Connecting with spirits can be a very loving and healing experience. I also made it clear that not everyone is destined to become a rescue medium.

This type of work is for those select few who can handle the tougher, heavier, and more emotional side of earthbound spirits. This unique field of mediumship is not easy. In fact, it can be rather difficult, annoying, frustrating, scary, emotional, and exhausting. I can't begin to mention how many times I swore off rescue work, cursed at my spiritual team, even yelled at spirits and wished I had never become a medium. I had wanted to experience the warm and fuzzy side of mediumship, and my guides were determined that I follow another path. The life of rescue work was my destiny. Yes, I had a choice. The choice was hard, a choice that I continually walked away from in the past. But I ultimately knew this was my journey and the right choice for me to make.

If you're reading this and feel a strong pull to rescue work, then you know it's the right choice for you. I'm not going to lie and say that it will be easy, because it won't be. Many people will try to persuade you and make you believe that what you are doing is wrong. They may make you feel that any spirits that have emotional issues are bad, or that their energy is heavy because they want to hurt people. As in life, there is the urge to judge a book by its cover and avoid what is perceived to only be negative. A great many spiritual and non-spiritual people alike will not understand this work and, therefore, will turn their backs on it.

Rescue mediumship has been misunderstood in the past, mainly due to modern society's conditional negative opinions of ghosts. My advice is this; don't let it stop you. Continue with your training and work. You need to understand that your role as a rescue medium is important. Don't let others cloud your judgement.

So if you're ready to start developing, training, and working as a rescue medium in the field of spirit rescue, please read on. I have tried to ensure that as much valuable information as possible is contained within. Take away what you want from the book and use what feels right to you. Everyone is unique and that difference is what makes you special. Just remember to work from a place of hope and healing, and everything will fall into place. I wish you luck in your journey. God Bless.

CHAPTER ONE

What Is a Rescue Medium?

What is a Rescue Medium? It's a question I'm asked all the time. The funny thing is that most people already have an idea of what rescue mediumship is through the media, including television shows and movies. They just didn't know there was a professional name for it and a structure to it that defines a rescue medium from a psychic medium. Rescue mediums specialize in communicating with earthbound spirits, counseling them regarding their issues, and guiding them through and aiding in their transition.

The field of rescue mediumship is growing due to the evolution of spirit work and our greater understanding of our connection to spirits and the spiritual plane. Our world is changing, and because of that, the greater consciousness is changing, allowing us to be more sensitive to the spirit world around us. We are now realizing that earthbound spirits (which are simply people in spirit that haven't made the full transition to the other side) are all around us, waiting, searching, and longing for the path that will take them into the light. Just like us, they are people in need of help.

The role of a rescue medium is becoming increasingly more important than ever before, because we now understand that a portion of these earthbound spirits need those in the physical world to aid in their transition. Not all earthbound spirits need rescue mediums. Most will eventually find their way on their own; but we can't ignore the ones that need a little extra assistance.

So, how exactly do rescue mediums help earthbound spirits? Can't we just point them in the right direction and tell them to go into the light? The answer to that question depends on the reason why the spirit is earthbound. Constructive guidance with earthbound spirits depends on their level of awareness and emotional attachment.

For the most part, rescue mediumship consists of four main components when interacting with earthbound spirits. These four components are:

1. Communication
2. Counseling
3. Clearing
4. Guidance

The first part naturally is the actual communication with earthbound spirits. This is achieved through our mediumship and psychic abilities of clairvoyance (seeing), clairaudience (hearing), clairsentience (sensing), claircognizance (knowing), clairalience (smelling), and clairgustance (tasting). Each psychic and medium will have their own strengths and weaknesses pertaining to these "Clair" abilities. In a medium's training, these abilities must be developed and enhanced to form a strong link with spirits. As we communicate with individual spirits, we can begin to understand the circumstances of their deaths and the compelling reasons behind their decisions to stay earthbound. Did they die suddenly? Was it a tragic death? Were they with other people when they died? The circumstances of a person's death can alter their perception and literal reality, so it's best to know what their awareness level is before we start talking to them about crossing over.

While communicating with these earthbound spirits, we can learn many things about them when they were alive, such as information about relatives, friends, lovers, jobs, passions, hobbies, dreams, desires, and even addictions that the spirit had. All of these details help put the puzzle pieces together while analyzing how we are going to help this spirit in their situation. Also, it is important to remember that communication styles can differ depending on culture and religion. By understanding the spirits' background, mediums can anticipate how receptive they will be to attempted communication.

The second part of rescue work is counseling. Once we've determined why the spirit is earthbound and how receptive they will be to communication we can develop ways to help them overcome emotional issues, attachments, or obstacles in their perception of their situation.

Counseling or support can be completed in several different ways depending on their emotional state. For instance, some spirits just need a gentle nudge of encouragement because they weren't ready to transition into light at the time of their death, while others require several days of emotional counseling and support to help them cope with a tragic death. If someone died in a very traumatic way, their thoughts and emotions could still be connected to the event of their death, which may not make them receptive to help. In other simpler situations, spirits just need comfort of the living to help them through their transition, so counseling will act more like just having a friendly conversation. Many more types of counseling methods will be discussed later in this book.

The next form of rescue work comes into play when you are aware that the spirit is not ready to move into the light and will need to be cleared away from populated areas until they have resolution of their issues. On most occasions, spirits that are earthbound will keep to themselves and prefer to be away from people who might interrupt their energy vibration. Though these earthbound spirits crave the comfort of familiar places and desire to be around people, the heavy physical presence of the living might overstimulate their energy. Quite often spirits will come out when the heavy and busy energy has lightened up a bit to allow them to roam around. At that time people may notice these spirits, but the spirit hasn't been disruptive and, if anything, creates a bit of entertainment for the residents/workers.

There are also times when spirits may become angry or resentful, which can lead to harassing the living. During these times the people residing or working in that area might feel uncomfortable with the spirit around. Rescue mediums then must work more as clearers in these circumstances. The rescue medium would be called into the area to explain to the spirit that if they do not stop the harassment, they will be removed. Usually these types of spirits aren't receptive to this agreement, especially if they are emotionally compromised, which is why several clearing techniques will be used to secure the area and remove the spirit.

Not only can spirits remain attached to places and objects, but they can also become attached to people. This is what is commonly called a "spirit attachment." Rescue Mediums act as clearers to help remove spirits from a person's energy through various clearing techniques that are described later in this book.

The last form of rescue mediumship is through guidance by aiding in the spirit's transition. Helping a spirit transition to the other side is more complex than you might think. It can take time through counseling to help raise the vibration of the earthbound spirit enough to be aware of the white light, depending on the spirit's personal situation. As I mentioned in *Toward the Light*, the light is always there, it's just hidden from the spirit's perception due to their vibration level and awareness. In order to bring in the white light, you must change the spirit's perception and realign their energy to the higher vibration of the white light. Opening up a door filled with white light to walk through might be the best analogy, but remember this is after we've communicated with them and counseled them enough to be ready for their transition.

Another way some rescue mediums help a spirit move into the light is by bringing in friends, family, or guides to help them pass onto the other side. Often spirits are greeted by these spiritual loved ones upon their death, though they aren't always aware of this. Lingering emotional issues can sometimes cloud the perception of the spirit making it difficult to connect with their guides. Rescue mediums will link these spiritual guides and the earthbound spirit together so that their guides can lead the earthbound spirit to the other side.

CHAPTER TWO
Your Spiritual Team

It's especially important to know that throughout your development and work in rescue mediumship, you will be working with your spiritual team. Your spiritual team consists of a great variety of gifted spiritual beings who each have their own devoted way of working with you. For the most part, your team will consist of spiritual beings such as ascended masters, guides, teachers, protectors, gatekeepers, shepherding spirits, healers, and messengers. Everyone's team will be different depending on their level of development, awareness of information, responsibility, purpose of their work, and personal choices. Working in the field of rescue mediumship, you will need to have a strong connection with your spiritual team and work often with them in order to help aid in an earthbound spirits' transition.

Before you try to identify who is on your personal spiritual team, it's best to clearly define who works on them, what their purpose is, and how they connect in with you. It's best to start at the top and work your way down so that you get a clearer picture of the levels of spiritual beings. The levels of your spiritual team can best be described as an inverted pyramid.

Divine Energy

At the very top of our inverted pyramid, only the purest Divine energy exists, which we call "God." Some would call this "Infinite Intelligence," "Supreme Being," "The One," "The Creator," "I AM," etc. Whichever name you feel connected to, use it. Each religion or culture will have name associations for God. God is the alpha and omega, the creator of all, the purest and highest form of all energy in existence. As I like to say, God above all. We all have our own personal connection to God, yet we are all connected to God as one. Everyone and everything is connected to God as one unit, yet we maintain our individuality when connecting to God. God is the force in which you should always feel connected to in your spiritual development. God is within you always. You'll never be left without this connection.

Ascended Masters

The second level down on the inverted pyramid of your spiritual team would be what we call ascended masters. Now, although I know there are other levels of spiritual beings under God, we are mainly discussing our personal spiritual team in connection to rescue work, so let's keep it simple with a divine order of hierarchy.

Ascended masters are spiritually enlightened beings who in past incarnations were humans, but who have undergone a series of spiritual transformations. These spiritual masters raised their vibration and consciousness to such a state as to have cleared all their karma. These masters come in to serve a greater and higher consciousness around the world as well as guide and support all of humanity in their ascension. You would call upon these spiritual masters for dealings of worldly issues such as war, peace, suffering, political issues, environmental disasters, etc. There is a long list of Ascended Masters, but some names you would be familiar with are: Jesus, Krishna, Mary Magdalen, Mother Mary, St. Germaine, Lady Nada, Ganesh, MA'at, Omega, and Vesta. I suggest you look up information on ascended masters for more information on their ascension process. Ways that these Masters work with you is through your emotions such as love and compassion. Working on a deeper and more spiritual level will invoke the energy of ascended masters. As a rescuer, you will be supporting a greater spiritual purpose by helping a spirit continue on with their journey into healing and ascension. This is when ascended masters will influence the energy around your work depending on what is needed at the time.

Archangels

The level of the ascended masters is usually shared with another energy form known to us as Archangels. Since I view archangels to be the highest form of angelic energy, I believe them to be just under God, alike the ascended masters. Archangels serve a greater purpose under God for the support of all humanity. According to most teachers, including Christian theologians, there are seven original archangels in the hierarchy. As you expand into new age theories and spiritual practices, you will find a longer list of archangels. I recommend studying more on archangels at your convenience to gain a greater understanding of their purpose and how you can call upon them. Some of the most well-known archangels in the spiritual community are:

MICHAEL

(Who is like God). Michael is considered to sit at the right side of God. Michael is known for his warrior strength and is recognized to be the Guardian of the Orthodox Faith and a fighter against heresies. He is the commander under God, who holds in his right hand a spear with which he attacks Satan and in his left hand a green palm branch. He is a defender and protector of all that is pure. Michael is considered to be one of the strongest forms of protection against negative energy. Colors associated with Michael differ between scholars. Some state Michael is red and gold while others claim Michael to manifest with colors of deep purple, gold, and blue.

GABRIEL

(God is my strength or Might of God). Gabriel is known to be at the left side of God. He/She is the archangel known to appear in male and female form. Gabriel is known as the patron saint of communication and mysteries. Also known as the messenger of God, Gabriel helps Earthly messengers such as teachers, counselors, writers, artists, and actors. Gabriel comes through with colors of copper, silver, and blue.

RAPHAEL

(It is God who heals). Raphael is known for healing and will bring in healing light from God. Raphael manifests with the color emerald green.

URIEL

(God is my light). Uriel enlightens our minds with ideas, solutions, and inspirations. Uriel can appear with the color yellow.

ARIEL

(Lion of God). Ariel is known to be the angel of nature. Ariel oversees the healing and protection of plants and animals as well as Earth's elements of air, water, and fire. Ariel comes through with the color of pale pink.

RAGUEL

(Friend of God). Raguel is known as the angel of vengeance, justice, fairness, and harmony. Raguel heals misunderstandings between foes and friends to form a harmonious relationship. Raguel will appear with the color pale blue.

CHAMUEL

(He who sees God). Chamuel is known for bringing peace into relationships as well as inner peace. Chamuel comes through with the color light green.

HANIEL

(Joy of God). Haniel is a spiritual guide for those with intuitive gifts. Haniel brings guidance in imagination and creativity. Haniel is known as the angel of joy. Haniel appears with the color blue.

AZRAEL

(Angel of Death). Azrael is the loving force that guides souls to the other side. Unfortunately, Azrael has been characterized by many folklores to be a dark, mysterious being that collects souls. Azrael is nothing of the sort, and if anything, serves as a radiating light of God that shines the path to heaven. Azrael works with the energy of death and transition. As a rescuer, you will work heavily with Azrael. Azrael manifests with the color cream white.

RAZIEL

(Secrets of God). Raziel is known to be the keeper of secrets and wisdom. Raziel is called upon when searching for spiritual wisdom within your soul. Raziel is also known to heal those with deep wounds of the soul that prevent us from finding inner peace and blocking us from our life purpose. Raziel appears with rainbow colors.

ZADKIEL

(Righteousness of God). Zadkiel is the patron angel of forgiveness. Zadkiel is a very important angel to rescue work, and you may call upon the energy of Zadkiel to aid lost souls looking for forgiveness. Zadkiel manifests with the color indigo blue.

Specialized Entities

The third level down on your spiritual team pyramid consists of spiritual entities that specialize in certain traits that oversee spiritual guidance, laws, healing, and messages within the universe. Within the spiritual level of hierarchy, entities such as seraphim, cherubim, thrones, dominions, virtues, powers, principalities, and angels play significant roles within your realm of rescue work. Most of the time, you will not know you are working with these entities because they channel through you naturally. You might feel an energy source around you while you work or you might feel inspired by their energy intention while you rescue. I found it's not especially important to know each entity that is working with you, as long as it's serving a purpose of love and healing. Just a brief note on each entity.

SERAPHIM

The highest order of the highest hierarchy are the seraphim, the celestial beings said to surround the throne of God, singing the music of the spheres, and regulating the movement of the heavens as it emanates from God.

CHERUBIM

Cherubine are known as the guardians of light and of the stars. They are part of the divinity that filters down from God.

THRONES

They are the companion angels of the planets. The Earth throne would be the guardian of our world.

DOMINIONS

The dominions are the heavenly beings who govern the activities of all the angelic groups beneath them.

VIRTUES

Virtues send out waves of divine energy throughout the world.

POWERS

Powers are the keepers of the conscience of all of humanity.

PRINCIPALITIES

Guardians of all large groups, they are also known as integration angels.

ANGELS

Angels are the guardians, healers, and protectors that serve humanity.

Teachers and Mentors

The fourth level down on the pyramid consists of teachers and mentors. This can include angels, while others are humans who have ascended to a higher spiritual level and can serve as teachers and guides. These teachers serve humanity in all forms of intellect, wisdom, and lessons. The mentors are the guides that provide service through your actions. So, teachers will provide the lesson while mentors will help walk you through the lesson. These teachers and mentors have a level of hierarchy depending on their own knowledge, wisdom, and level of ascension. In the spirit world, the color of their spiritual aura defines the ascension level and purpose for these teachers. Depending on the spiritual studies that have been done and the information received through various hypnotic studies, the level of hierarchy is purple at the top, then deep blue, light blue, green, gold, yellow, then white at the lowest. Now, depending on the subject to be learned, teachers may come from various backgrounds, such as intellectual, emotional, physical, or spiritual realms. Many teachers may have been geniuses in another life and have come to serve you through their knowledge and intelligence. Other teachers may be Saints and provide inspirational teachings of love and compassion, or knowledge in spiritual endeavors. Yet other teachers may have been great warriors and will teach you strength and bravery. All are skilled and can be extremely helpful.

Healers and Supporters

The fifth level of the pyramid is occupied by the healers and supporters. These would be the ones to call to through prayer in times of need. Shepherding spirits, angels, shamans, etc., would be among this group. I also like to think of this level as the spiritual working class. These beings work heavily through humanity servicing many different needs. Channeling these spiritual healers through Reiki, hands-on healing, inspirational speeches, counseling, nursing, emergency services, spirit work, etc., would be beneficial as these spirits work alongside the living for these purposes. In rescue work, you will find yourself working closely with almost all spiritual healers and supporters as this is the main focus of your work. Individual healers will make themselves known to you when they offer their services and support to you.

Protectors and Guides

The sixth level down consists of your personal protectors, healers, guides, and animal guides. These spiritual helpers work with you and your soul group when you need guidance, strength, protection, healing, inspiration, comfort, and love. The list really goes on with the type of work that they do with you and your group. They are your full support from the spirit world. Whenever you need help working out a situation, they are there. When you need to be calm through a stressful situation, they are there. When you need healing through a sickness, be it mental or physical, they are there. Anytime you are in need that doesn't interfere with your free will or life lessons, they are and will always be there for you. These spiritual helpers oversee all energy work in your personal soul group. Your soul group is like your spiritual family that studies, learns, and ascends together in between various lives. Many people speculate on how many souls are in your soul group. Some say seven, some say twenty-four, some say 144. I really don't think there is a magical number to this. It should naturally fluctuate as spirits ascend. I do know that most souls in a soul group stay at a pretty close vibration to their soul mates. If one moves up, then the rest are inspired to ascend as well. It's said that you will know when you meet someone from your close soul group as you will feel a strong connection to this person as if you've known them your whole life and feel extremely close to them. There are many people who have never met anyone else from their soul group. Contrary to popular belief, soul mates can be of either sex, not just the opposite sex as often portrayed in the media. Also, souls may stay behind to be the healers and supporters of other members of their soul group. There are no rules, just love and support. Oftentimes spiritual helpers in this group would be members of your family like your mother, father, grandparents, etc. These spirits will come in from time to time to help you out and provide moral support. They can't interfere as much as the main healers and guides from your soul group, but they will come in and serve you throughout your life if you accept them. Don't be surprised if a family member is a soul from your soul group. It's typical for soul mates to stay close during a lifetime and be reincarnated within the same family.

Your Guide

The seventh and final level of your spiritual team pyramid would be your personal main guide or angel. As we incarnate back into life, we are given personal guides and angels that work only with us. These would be your main guide, personal angel, and power animal. It's best that you learn who these spiritual beings are as you will do most of your work with them. They will walk beside you through every situation in your life. They are the main support through your soul's life mission and purpose. Many great spiritual teachers and mediums will tell you to ask for Archangel Michael's help or ask for Saint Theresa to come in and guide you, and so on. They expect you to go straight to the top of the hierarchy to directly address issues going on in your life. This is great advice, but why go all the way to the top and skip several levels of guides, healers, protectors, and friends on the way? Why not ask for help from personal guides and protectors when you are in need? Quite often your personal guides will channel the energy of the great masters to you when you ask for their assistance, so you are getting the energy transfer whether you know it or not. So it's often wise not to always go straight to the top. You're missing out on a tremendous amount of personal assistance.

Now that you know the levels of hierarchy with your spiritual team, its best to understand how to work with them. Everyone working in the spiritual field has their own way of connecting in with their own team. There are those who have been doing it since childhood without realizing it, while some have just begun to connect in with their team. For the most part, there are a few common ways that spiritual guides, healers, teachers, and protectors come through to you.

Dreams

The dream world, or as others would call it, the dream state, is a powerful tool to connecting you to your spiritual helpers. In this state of awareness, you are somewhere in between the conscious and unconscious realm where information can be exchanged. It's said that your soul makes contact with your ego and mind at this time to transfer needed information into your consciousness. Your spiritual team can do the same at this time. Usually your guides will help you during the day through feelings, but it's during the dream state that they can send images, feelings, messages, and concerns to you. I would recommend keeping a dream journal next to your bed to write down information that you receive while you dream. This could be information like where you were in your dream, what you were doing, who you were talking to, and so on. Try to write down as much as you can remember, as most dreams have a way of slipping out of your mind only moments after waking. If you had a very profound dream that seemed so real that it really affected you emotionally, then be sure to write it down and talk to someone about it. Most likely it was a strong message trying to get through.

Guided Meditation

I believe guided meditation is one of the best ways to contact your spiritual team. Guided meditation can help you achieve altered states of consciousness, much like your dream state, only while you are awake. It can take some time to quiet your mind enough to reach this state of awareness because some people have a hard time "turning it off." This means their mind never stops thinking, "Did I do the dishes? When are the folks coming for dinner? Did I pay my bills? How am I going to finish this project?" and so on. You must learn to distance yourself from everyday worries and thoughts to reach a state of inner peace and tranquility. For some of us, including myself, I learned how to mediate while doing mediocre chores like dishes, vacuuming, folding laundry, and yes . . . driving (sorry). I can't tell you how many times I start to meditate while driving only to find myself exactly where I was supposed to be fifteen minutes later without realizing that I've been driving on a road with twists and turns, stop lights, and other cars. I'm sure many people can relate to this everyday activity. I know I must have a very strong driving guide on my team. Thank goodness! But for those who have a hard time meditating, I recommend a guided meditation as a start. This helps focus your mind onto something while you learn to quiet the rest of your physical and spiritual bodies. And don't worry if it takes time to meet a guide at first. Sometimes seeing colors, hearing sounds, or feeling vibrations is enough to know that they are trying to get through. Keep doing the meditation, and I promise you that it will eventually connect you to your guides.

Inner Voices and Feelings

This is a big one for me since I have had my guides talking to me from a very early age. These voices came through my own inner mind, so I had no idea that these were guides talking to me. For those of us with strong clairaudience ("clear hearing"), these voices will be very strong and powerful. You may even get feelings when you hear the voices. It's sort of like feeling the words at the same time you hear them. If a guide tells you to "calm down and trust yourself," you may get a feeling of comfort and support all around you while you hear the words. That's how some guides can connect to you when you are awake. The feelings and voices will usually come from within yourself, kind of like you're talking to yourself. Don't shrug off these gut feelings or words in your head. These voices and feelings are a gift from your guides when they feel you need extra help. Learn how to trust it when it happens and be grateful for your guides' help.

Spiritual Signs and Messages

While developing your gifts of intuition and mediumship, your guides and spiritual helpers will try to come through to you on a non-physical level as explained above through dreams, feelings, and voices. They also like to manifest physical signs as well to get your attention. I've had many experiences in my past of receiving signs and messages when new guides, angels, or masters are ready to work with me. Some of these signs and messages would be:

- Hearing the same name over and over again.
- Seeing symbols like feathers, rocks, or crystals that really draw your attention.
- Hearing songs or watching movies that have a distinctive message to them.
- Having certain animals come to you over and over again.
- Feeling drawn to certain books.
- Seeing colors or images repeatedly.

These are all ways that spiritual helpers are trying to get through. If you feel drawn to something, pay attention to what the message is or what the main theme is for it. People often find that if they receive these physical clues, they can specify in meditation if the message was received. Don't be afraid to ask questions to your guides or request more clarity. For example, one of my experiences of a guide coming in to work with me was through a name, a color, and a song. I had a few friends in the psychic community mention the name St. Germain to me on occasion, but I really didn't know anything about St. Germain. Not only did they mention his name, but also psychics began telling me that I had a violet color energy around me whenever they gave me a reading. Again, it was not enough for me to pay attention to as violet is usually around me when I do spirit work, and most of my friends talk about Saints and angels frequently. It wasn't until I started hearing the song "Say Geronimo" that it began to click. I really liked this song even though the message of the song didn't mean anything to me. Every time this song came on, I felt compelled to listen to it, and I felt connected to it. In the song they say the words "say Geronimo," but in my mind, I kept hearing Saint Geronimo. I knew it wasn't the right lyrics, but somehow my mind wanted to hear the word Saint instead. So, I began researching Saint Geronimo. Nothing solid came up that I could make a connection to, but then I remembered what my friends had been saying about Saint Germain before and it began to make sense. That possibly I was being persuaded to look up information on Saint Germain. I suddenly felt an intense feeling that I was on the right path. Why did it take a song about another name to connect me to Saint Germain? I honestly don't know. It is possible because I feel drawn to music, and my guides like working with me that way. So, all three messages involved music, hearing the same name through various people, and the color violet playing a part to clue me in that Saint Germain was ready to work with me. The same can work for you. You just need to pay attention to the subtle clues.

False Guides

In the field of rescue mediumship, we need to be even more on guard about who may be coming through to communicate with us. Other mediums that communicate with spirits on the other side may have situations from time to time when a mischievous spirit may come through. However, they certainly do not get the type of spirit influence that rescue mediums receive because of the vibrational energy that they work within. Working as a rescue medium you will be faced with several energy levels from various energy sources. These can range from a lost earthbound spirit looking for healing, a child molester looking for redemption and guidance, to lower level energies such as negative energy manifestation. Rescuers work at a lower level so that we may raise these energies up. Do not think that you are negative because of this; instead think of yourself as being strong enough and bright enough to go down this far to heal those in need and come back up. Because of this, we need to be secure in our work, more than most mediums. You may come across various spirits that will try to confuse you, manipulate your emotions, and trick you into believing that they are your guides, angels, or family on the other side. They may come through very loving at first and will try to gain your trust. You must learn over time the differences between these spirits and your true spirit team. It can take time, especially if you're just starting out. Your guides may take a step back to have you learn through this challenge. They believe that you cannot learn everything through classes or channeled information. There are some things that can only be learned through experience. To make things a little easier for some of you, I've listed several hints that may help signal to you that these spirits are not your true guides. These include but are not limited to:

- Promises that feed into your ego.
- Misguided information.
- Information that pushes you away from friends and family.
- Anger or frustration with you when you won't listen to them.
- Pushing you into doing something you feel to be uncomfortable.
- Telling you what to do all the time.
- Inappropriate energy direction (touching or sexual stimulation).
- Heavy pressure around you when they talk to you.

Learning how your true guides communicate with you is key to being secure in your spirit work. For the most part, guides and angels will speak through you, not to you. If you feel that you are being misguided, raise your vibration and clear yourself. When in doubt, trust your gut instincts. Pay attention to how you feel. Remain calm, and know that your real guides are standing by to help. Always.

CHAPTER THREE
Asking for Signs

Working with spirits, guides, and angels isn't easy at first. It takes time to get used to trusting the signs and signals from your spiritual helpers to know if you are truly communicating or not. Doubt will get in the way from opening up and believing in your connection to spirit or your spiritual team, so it's best to ask for a little assistance while developing your skills, which will help put your mind at ease.

I remember when I first started developing my mediumship ability. I was so in doubt that I had the ability to communicate with spirits that I needed definitive proof that this was indeed happening. I had always heard voices in my head since I was very young and had always attributed this to my "inner voice" or subconscious mind talking to me. I would never have imagined that it was spirits or guides communicating with me from an outside source. These "voices" or information I heard always came from within me. So how was I to believe that this was coming from something other than myself?

But why was I answering my own questions or calming myself down when I got upset? How did I know exactly what I needed to hear in times of need? How did I explain these unusual feelings of talking to someone even though I knew I was alone? I couldn't explain it, which is why I was so intrigued with the idea that these voices could be my guides, angels, or spirits trying to help and guide me.

These voices told me that they understood it was difficult for us here in the physical world to completely trust in this communication at first because of our strong connection to the physical communication styles that we use. So, in order for my guides and spirits to prove to me that they did exist, I needed to see physical signs or signals from them to prove that they were the voices that I'd been hearing.

Okay, let's just face it. I'm extremely stubborn. I know it, my guides know it, and I wasn't taking simple answers or signs to prove their existence. I needed, without a shadow of a doubt, a sign that these were indeed my guides, angels, or spirits trying to communicate with me. So what kind of sign or signal was I going to ask for? I had no idea. I didn't know what spirits could do from the other side, nor did I know what a guide was and what they could do. Could they mess with the lights? Could they talk through the radio? Could they appear to me in a physical form? I wasn't sure. So I had asked them. "What kind of sign are you talking about?" They said, "Anything that makes you believe." Well, let me think.

For some crazy reason I starting thinking about a movie that my dad loved because of his Jewish decent: *Fiddler on the Roof.* Now, this is a movie that you don't see around very often, so I asked them, "Why don't you show me something from this movie? If you do, I'll be more inclined to believe that you are real."

Well . . . that very night, my husband and I were talking about our day and things that had happened with the children. I had forgotten all about the conversation I'd had with my guides earlier that day. I had gotten so involved working around the house, my mind was not thinking about spirits, guides, or anything spiritual in nature at the time. For some reason, my husband started joking around and making fun of movies from his childhood. And what do you know, from out of the blue he starts joking around about the movie *Fiddler on the Roof.* I had to stop myself from what I was doing and think. Wait a minute! Was that the sign? Was that coming from my guides? How in the world can this sign come from my husband? I didn't mention anything to him as I didn't want to seem crazy, but I have to admit I was starting to feel that way. I brushed this off and thought to myself that it was just a coincidence and nothing more. How could this be the sign?

Later that night I heard those very familiar voices in my head.

Spirits: "So . . . did you get our sign?"

Amy: "How could that have been a sign? It was so small, I'm not convinced. How am I supposed to believe in something so simple as that?"

Spirits: "Well, what do you expect?"

Amy: "I don't know. I told you I was stubborn and that I needed something more than just someone joking around about the movie *Fiddler on the Roof.*"

Spirits: "Okay, you want something bigger?"

Amy: "Well yeah, I need something to really prove this to me. If you want me to believe, I need a big sign."

Spirits: "Okay."

And with that they fell silent and I shortly went to bed.

The next morning, I got up and went about the usual morning routine. I got in the car and started driving the children to school before I went to work. The road I drive every day to get to the school is only two lanes. On each side of the street are buildings like gas stations, insurance offices, and such. And wouldn't you know while driving down the road to school I look up and see a huge banner hanging across both lanes. It was directly above me and was clearly seen from anyone driving on the road. And what do you think was written on that banner? *Fiddler on the Roof* was now playing at the local opera house. I was speechless.

Are you kidding me? I was just on this same road the day before and there wasn't any sign there. The banner just happens to show up the day after I ask for this particular sign from spirit. I asked myself, "How is this possible? "Well?" Spirits responded, "You asked for a big sign." Yes, I did, but this was a huge banner across the road that was unmistakably clear to everyone that *Fiddler on the Roof* was coming to town. This was the first time I realized how powerful messages can be delivered by the other side. It wouldn't be the only message I received that day.

After I dropped the children off, I drove into work with a level of shock that I still feel to this day. I walked into work and saw the community newspaper on my desk. I open up the newspaper and on the very first page that I open to, there's a bold advertisement: "*Fiddler on the Roof*, now playing at the Opera House." "Okay, okay, you made your point," I said to myself. To this day I still can't believe it, though I saw it with my own two eyes as did my family. How did spirits do this? Did they put this thought in my mind? Did I psychically know the show was coming to town? Who knows? All I know is that this was not a coincidence anymore. Those voices I've been hearing all my life were now becoming an outside source communicating to me through my thoughts. And I had been doing this for years without even knowing!

I was now beginning to believe. Yes, it had taken a huge, overwhelmingly obvious sign from my guides to prove this to me. But I believed, without a doubt . . . and it was wonderful. It was as though everything was suddenly clear; it finally made sense. From that point on, I started communicating back to these voices when I heard them, and we started having great conversations.

With all this being said, I'm not telling all of you to start asking for huge signs from your guides, angels, and spirits to make you believe. Just know that they can provide signs to you when they know you are in need. It doesn't take something big, maybe just a sound, an object, a song, or something being said to you. A sign can be many different things depending on what your guides think will work. Don't be afraid to push for something more if you aren't sure about your sign. The point of a sign is to put you at ease and help you believe that they are real and communicating with you. Also remember, signs are ways to help you open up and trust. Your guides won't keep giving you signs over and over again. At some point, you're going to need to trust. They will only provide signs when it's needed, not when it's wanted. But, feel free to ask. They're always around to communicate with you.

CHAPTER FOUR
Mediumship Development

By now you've noticed working as a rescue medium is much different than working as a psychic or spiritual medium. As a psychic medium, or what I like to call "message medium," you mainly work as a mediator or message bearer from spirit to the receiver. Psychic mediums train to raise their vibration, connect in with the spirit world, learn techniques and communication styles with spirit to validate personal information about the spirit, and relay messages to the living. Psychic mediumship is one of the best ways to validate the existence of life after death for so many people who are searching for answers about the afterlife. It also serves as a source of healing for people who are suffering through the loss of a loved one.

I also work as a psychic medium when I am not doing rescue work, as I love connecting people to spirits on the other side. I believe the validation of life after death is extremely important because it allows us to live without fear of the unknown after death. We can then understand a greater purpose to our lives and in turn help us strive to better ourselves by living our lives to their fullest. I like to think of it as a domino effect. If you understand that life exists after death, then you start to understand that we are all connected to a greater source beyond the existence of the physical world. By understanding that concept, we know that we are all connected on a spiritual level. If we are all connected on a spiritual level in a higher consciousness, then maybe we are all created from a higher source or creator life force. So if we are all connected to a creator life force that has expanded itself into different levels of consciousness and existences further and further throughout various forms of energy, then what else is out there?

So, mediumship is just one step in a long road of spiritual self-discovery. It takes baby steps, and I truly believe that our world is ready for these baby steps to take us further down that road of discovery. More and more people are awakening to the realization that we do continue on to another life form after the physical death. This is a huge step and one that we've been waiting to take for a long time.

Without any surprise, our roles as Rescue Mediums are growing due to this spiritual awakening. We are now noticing more and more earthbound spirits around us because we have raised our global energy vibration to a slightly higher rate, allowing us to view the energy of earthbound spirits more often. Connecting in with earthbound spirits through rescue mediumship is different and more in-depth than doing message mediumship. We aren't going to concentrate as much on the message work, unless it's warranted by the spirit for their transition. Rescue mediums work on mediumship skills that will help aid in a rescue or clear spirits away from people or places.

All necessary basic training in psychic development must be learned first before you start training as a medium. This would include learning about chakras, auras, energy vibration, "Clair" abilities, astral projection, meditation techniques, psychic protection, telepathy, psychometry, precognition, retro-cognition, affirmations, prayers, and so on. Mediumship is an expanded form of psychic ability that allows the sensitive person to raise their vibration to the spiritual world and connect within the scope of their ESP (extrasensory perception) abilities. So, having a firm foundation in psychic development is required before you learn about rescue mediumship. Not all psychics will have the ability to raise their vibration to the spirit world and serve as mediums. I think the notion that all psychics can be mediums is false. There are those who work better as psychics and those who work better as mediums. One isn't better than the other. Everyone has their own strengths. In fact, as a rescue medium, you're going to be using your psychic and mediumship abilities simultaneously, so strengthening both skills will be required.

The first step in your development for rescue work should be basic mediumship. Learn how to raise your vibration to spirit energy. You're not going to need to raise it too high because earthbound spirits reside at an energy level just above the vibration of the physical world. There are several levels of energy that mediums work within. You're going to become very familiar with each level so that you can understand who or what you are working with.

Planes of Existence

The seven primary levels of energy, or what we call planes of existence, that you will focus your attention on are the physical, astral, causal, akashic, mental, messianic, and logoic. You can and will connect to all levels within your work of rescue mediumship, but the three levels that you will work in more often are the physical, astral, and causal planes. You cannot reach one plane of existence without going through various levels in between. These levels of existence are usually overlapping, which creates an entirely different vibration in itself. This is a transitionary level where spirit energy can slowly ascend comfortably. It is in these transitionary levels where you will be doing most of your work aside from the three main levels.

First, you must understand the three main levels of existence for rescue work.

Physical

The physical plane is referred to as the visible reality of space, of time, of energy, and matter. It is the plane of existence where our astral body merges with our esoteric body (physical body). It is the plane where all energy manifests in physical form. Many people refer to this plane as the Earth plane, which is why many people call spirits that reside just above this plane earthbound spirits. Earthbound spirits typically reside in the transitional level between physical and Astral planes.

Astral

The Astral plane is the first non-physical plane where time and matter no longer exist. This energy vibration is faster than the speed of time and lighter than any form of matter. It is in this plane of existence that our soul makes its transition to the higher consciousness. This plane is what I believe is the plane in which global consciousness is experienced. The Astral plane is a multilayered, multidimensional environment that changes within the scope of individual perception. It's also the plane where astral bodies can regenerate, educate, work, and ascend to higher levels of existence. Angels, healers, lower dimensional teachers, guides, and what I call the "spiritual working class" all serve in this level. Many different teachings explain that there are seven different levels within the Astral plane. I'm not going to go into detail with names and definitions because you really aren't going to need all of the information, and it might seem confusing. So the best way to describe these different levels is by the emotional and mental state of the discarnate being. Lower levels of the Astral world will house spirits in need of healing, reconstruction, counseling, and self-discipline. These would be spirits that have made the full transition but still carry a heavy vibration due to their negative mental and emotional state. As you ascend to a higher vibration within the Astral world, you connect with spirits that have just reunited with family, friends, and their soul group. They also might be going through a life-review with their guides, so you won't be connecting with these spirits often since they will be very busy.

Higher vibrational levels would be spirits that are working with energy forces on the Earth plane. Healers, mentors, warriors, protectors, etc., that were recently carnate on Earth that want to serve others to relieve karma. They would be considered guides, helpers, or mentors of the physical world. Remember that I mentioned in the spiritual team section that mentors will come in to help walk you through a challenge? These sprits may have experienced the same challenge in their own life, and through helping you with your challenge their karma is cleared.

Causal

This plane of existence is known as the mental plane or the plane of thought. All of the experiences you've encountered, lessons learned, and successes through these experiences are stored in the casual mind. This is connected to a higher consciousness known as the Causal plane. Universal knowledge is stored and attained through this plane of existence. Teachers, guides, scholars, angels, and such reside in this plane with universal and spiritual knowledge and wisdom. This is where some of your guides reside. Their energy vibration has reached a state of a higher consciousness and wisdom that allows them to become teachers and supporters for spirits in the Physical and Astral planes.

These three levels will be the main source of your spirit work. As stated above, there are many levels of transition between these levels. So why is all this important? When developing your mediumship skills, you must learn how to differentiate between the types of spirits you work with depending on their vibrational level. Density and intensity will help you determine this.

Another part of your intuitive development should focus on reading energy. Energy flows through you and everything else in the universe. Our internal personal energy sources are what we call chakras. By opening and enhancing our chakras, we can help connect our energy to other energy vibrations like people, objects, and spirits. That's what most psychic work is about. Learning how to strengthen your energy so that you can connect to and read energy from other people, places, or things. All intuitive work is an energy transfer. I would start with psychometry, which is reading energy off of an object, to help you learn to read energy. Once you've learned how to pick up on sounds, images, feelings, and cognizance, then you would start raising your vibration each time you work to see what new information comes through and start reading that energy.

Chakras

The seven main chakras are the centers in our bodies in which energy flows through. In your early intuitive development, you should have learned about each of the seven chakras, their meanings, colors, and how to open each of them. These seven are: the root, sacral, solar plexus, heart, throat, third eye, and crown chakras. Below are the seven chakras, their basic meanings, and how they are used in your rescue work.

ROOT

This is located just under your body's torso at the base of your tailbone region. The root chakra is associated with the color red. It is your grounding energy. This relates to all physical matters of material, security, and survival instincts. Use this chakra to help ground your energy into Mother Earth. When opening your root chakra, imagine a red energy beam from your chakra moving down the ground, wrapping itself around a thick and solid root and stabilizing itself into Mother Earth's energy.

SACRAL

This is located in the pelvic region. The sacral chakra is associated with the color orange. This chakra regulates energy around family, relationships, your perception of the world. It also stimulates well-being, pleasure, and sexuality. This chakra needs to be cleared of any negative karma before you start doing rescue work.

SOLAR PLEXUS

This is located in your stomach region right around the belly button. The solar plexus chakra is associated with the color yellow. This chakra regulates the energy of feelings, gut instincts, intuition, self-worth, confidence, purpose, and motivation. This chakra will be used frequently in your rescue work when you read energy. Your intuition and feelings will be enhanced as you stimulate this chakra.

HEART

This is located in the center of your chest. It is associated with the color green. This chakra regulates energy around love, joy, and peace. It is used heavily in rescue work because we need to remember unconditional love when dealing with troubled spirits. Compassion, forgiveness, as well as empathetic and motivational energy will derive from this chakra.

THROAT

Located in the throat region, it is associated with the color light blue. This chakra regulates energy around communication, self-expression, and truth. This chakra is used mainly for communication purposes in rescue work. If your throat chakra is closed, then it would be hard to express your feelings and help inspire spirits.

THIRD EYE

This is located in the middle of your forehead. It is associated with the color indigo (dark bluish-purple). This chakra regulates energy of vision, sight, intuition, clarity, and wisdom. You will use this chakra heavily with your crown chakra in rescue work. Learning how to see and read energy imprints will be important in your clearing work.

CROWN

This is located just above the center of your head. It is associated with the color violet. This chakra regulates energy of our connection to spirit and the spirit world, regardless of the level of existence they reside in. I like to think of it as the door to spirit. This chakra, along with the third eye, will be used the most in your work.

Meditation

The last form of basic development in mediumship that should be studied is meditation. Meditation is a useful skill to learn to help raise your vibration to an altered state of consciousness. Meditation can take you to a heightened state to connect in with spiritual energy in higher planes of existence, or it can take you down to a very low subconscious state in which things lay dormant, hide, or where left forgotten. Meditation is a practice in which you can relax your mind and body for many different uses like healing, grounding, contemplation, learning, astral traveling, regression, resting, energy balancing, and so on. Meditation has so many beneficial uses that people in today's world are just beginning to explore the possibilities. The best way to start learning how to meditate is through a group meditation, video meditation, or audio meditation session. Having someone walk you through a guided meditation is useful to help learn how to quiet your mind and focus on the moment at hand. Learning to shut out the outside world and one's daily thoughts can take time, so be patient. For those who have done meditation in the past, concentration on reaching heightened states to the spirit world should be focused.

Listed below are steps that should be taken to prepare for a meditation as well as a guided meditation you can use to help connect you to your guides.

STEP 1: Prepare

Take a moment in the day when you know that you have about thirty minutes or longer to yourself without any distractions. For early morning risers, try to stick to a morning meditation, for those who are night owls, try to do yours late at night. It's best to stick to a time of day when you aren't tired and drained from daily concerns. Try to find a place in your home where you can be comfortable. Is this your bed, a couch, the floor, or a nice comfy chair? If you're going to be on the floor, place a nice comfortable mat under you so that you do not feel the friction from the hard floor. Whichever you feel you can relax the most in, use it. Avoid wearing tight fitting clothes, and take off your shoes if you can. Put on some relaxing music, preferably without lyrics. There is a great selection of meditation music online that is free. Use it! Light a few candles, place a few crystals out that help enhance the energy you are trying to connect with. Use healing crystals if you are trying to relax, restore, and refresh. High vibrational crystals if you are trying to connect to the spirit world. Dark and grounding crystals if you are trying to go deep into the subconscious, and so on. Next, light some incense or smudge the room if you like to help neutralize the energy and to set your thought and intent. Many cultures or religions like to place offerings out on the alter before they meditate to their guides. Some offerings might include a glass of wine, some food, or even flowers. Again, this isn't necessary; these are just suggestions to prepare for a great meditation and to invite your ancestors, guides, angels, and spiritual family in to connect.

STEP 2: Protection and Energy Stimulation

Whenever I begin my meditations, I call in my spiritual guides that help protect and secure my energy so that I am completely at ease. Protection should never seem like you are fighting against something. Rather, it should be a continual tool to use to secure your environment for a peaceful meditation. The best ways to protect your energy other than using crystals, incense, music, and candles is by personal energy stimulation. When you are in a comfortable position, begin to pay attention to your breathing. Take a deep breath in and exhale. Feel your body relax when you do this. Take a second breath in. This time, when you breathe in, imagine breathing in positive and loving energy, and when you breathe out, you are pushing out any dense, heavy, and negative energy. Push all your worries away. Take a third breath in and do the same thing until you start feeling lighter and lighter. After the first three breaths you should start to feel centered and ready to move on.

Breathe normally and try to relax. You will begin the energy vibration stimulation by activating your chakras. Imagine your chakras as balls of energy that align up through the center of your body. As we open and stimulate each ball of energy, you enhance your energy around you, making it easier to connect to other forms of energy. Start with the root chakra which is located at the base of your spine and image a red ball of energy opening up like the bud of a flower that opens up to the shining sun. Allow this energy to open, expand and radiate all around you. Feel grounded and secure in your environment.

At this time imagine a ray of red light from this chakra grounding down into the energy of Mother Earth. Wrap this ray of red light around a deep root in Mother Earth, allowing Earth energy to flow up through this energy source into your chakra. This is your grounding. Thank Mother Earth for her energy and healing. As we continue on our journey up through our chakras we move into the sacral chakra. This is the color orange. Again, imagine this energy source opening up like a bud of a flower in the sun, radiating its energy all around you. Do the same for each chakra moving up the energy flow through your body. With each chakra you open, you should feel lighter and lighter with loving spirit energy around you. When you get to the crown chakra, open this violet energy source and expand this energy all around you reaching far up into the spirit world.

When I mediate, I like to go up one more chakra above the crown to the chakra connected to divine energy. This color is white with a golden hue. Imagine this chakra opening up and expanding its energy all around you. As we connected in our root chakra down into Mother Earth, we will connect this divine chakra down into our body to connect into a higher consciousness. Imagine this white energy chakra shinning down a ray of white light that penetrates down into your crown chakra, encircling it with golden white light. Imagine this white light penetrating and encircling all your chakras within your body, just like your crown chakra. By doing this, your internal energy is now protected. Start to imagine your white chakra above your crown radiate a glowing, bright, white light around you that encircles your body. Imagine this circulating light radiating all around you and protecting you from the top of your head down to your feet. This is your shield. When you imagine your shield around you, give gratitude to the loving energy of the divine. Ask for your spiritual protectors, healers, teachers, power animals, and guides to come through to be with you. Ask for four angels to come in and protect the four corners of your room. This is an outside shield for energy that may come in from outside the house or building. Give thanks to the elemental energies of the North, South, East, and West for their protection and energy.

Send out love to your spiritual team. Invite them in so that you may know them and communicate with them. Allow only those of the highest and best to come through. Even though we as rescuers work with energies that are not always in the highest and best due to their vibration, most meditations are used to raise your vibration to connect into your spiritual team for knowledge, guidance, and healing. We are only looking to connect to high vibrations at this time.

STEP 3: Meditation

Once you've expanded your energy field by opening your chakras, raising your vibration, protecting your energy with the white light, and calling in your spiritual team, you may begin to move into your meditation or journey.

Sense, feel, or imagine yourself in a sacred space that is special to you. This may be a field of flowers, a cliff by the ocean, a big oak tree expanding out to the sky, a river or creek to sit by, and so on. Go where you feel most at peace. This is your starting point for your meditation.

Sit and enjoy your surroundings. Feel the soft breeze on your face, smell and hear the roar of the ocean. Use what works best with your personality to help put you in the right frame of mind for guidance. Above you, imagine the sun shining down. Look up and feel the soft, warm glow of the sun on your face. When I meditate I imagine this light from the sun to be the light of God, shining love all over me. Let this shining light make you feel loved and cherished. Begin to invite your guides in by sending out thoughts to them. Let them know that you are ready to connect. Pay attention to small changes around you.

Does someone approach you? Do animals come up to you? Does a road show itself before you, or does your body float up to reach for universal cosmic knowledge? Your spiritual guides and angels will come in and help guide you through this meditation to your unique personality. If someone comes up to talk to you, listen. If a road shows itself before you, walk it. If a boat floats up to the water you are sitting next to, ride it. Everything will guide you further along in your meditation. Always remember what comes through to you, because your guides will use symbols to relay messages to you in meditation. Objects, animals, colors, sounds, feelings, etc., are all symbols. Over time, you will learn what each symbol means, which will help explain to you what message your guides are trying to tell you.

If you aren't familiar with meditation and have a hard time going off on your own, listen to a guided meditation and follow the flow of directions from your speaker. Depending on the meditation, you may meet your guides, you may be brought to a place of learning, or you may be greeted by friends or family. Each meditation takes you further along with your spiritual journey. Meditation not only helps you receive information from your guides, but it also helps you learn how to raise your vibration and connect in with spirit energy, which are ways to help you connect in with universal wisdom and guidance.

CHAPTER FIVE

Emotional and Mental Conditioning

Building emotional strength will be one of your greatest assets in rescue work. Earthbound spirits are not always easy to work with, and dealing with their emotional issues can be very draining and disturbing at times. There may be situations when you have to face a mother who has killed all her children and herself. You may have to face a man who blew up a building, killing multiple people including himself. Other situations may require you to help a young girl who was molested and murdered or a soldier killed in combat. These can be very stressful situations that need emotional strength to work through.

We have to remember that some of these spirits are earthbound for negative reasons, and we need to be on guard at all times. Yes, it's true that we serve as healers and guides for these spirits, but they can take advantage of you, lie, harass, or even attack you—which is why you need to have really thick skin in this field of mediumship. Those who are more fragile with their emotions can be easily compromised, and this is why I tell them to stay away from spirit rescue. A great many mediums will tell you that it's best to stay away from negative spirits, but since this is your job and you will deal mainly with these negative issues, it's best that I explain how and why these spirits can affect you.

EGO

As much as your guides want you to feel special, they rarely try to fluff your ego and create an environment for you to expand your popularity. If your guides feel you have a greater purpose in your life, such as becoming a famous medium or inspirational speaker, they will usually caution about your ego and focus your attention on healing and spiritual matters for greater consciousness. Serving your community or the country may take you down a road of notoriety, but your guides will usually remind you of your service to spirit as your reason for doing so.

As stated before, earthbound spirits may falsify their connection to you by explaining that they are guides. There are spirits that may have wished to become popular themselves and try to experience this through you. Other negative and more devious spirits will try to feed into your ego by stimulating your need to be important and special. They claim that only through your popularity will you be happy in what you do. Feeding you false information to make you believe in something that isn't true can take you down a long road of disappointment and frustration, which is exactly what these spirits want. They wish to build you up for the big fall. Think of it as the bully who pretends to like you and makes you think that others will like you because you're so special, then he/she will embarrass you in front of everyone to show you that it was all fake and that no one will ever like you. These bullies exist in the spirit world, and you have to learn how to detect them. It's not always easy. Spirits can be experts at manipulating you through your emotions and thoughts. They find your weaknesses and play off them like a game. It's only through your faith in what you do and your connection to your true spiritual team that will help you through this situation.

Obsessions and Addictions

Obsessions and addictions can hinder us here in the physical world. Quite often, we find ourselves struggling with mental disorders that we would normally hide from others. As humans, we aren't perfect; many of us suffer through painful situations that lead us to do things that aren't for our highest good or best. Obsessions are a temporary mental handicap that allow our mind to believe in something that may or may not be true. We believe so heavily in something because it feels so right to us, that we fail to recognize logical reasoning. This is where spirits can gain control. They can manipulate your mind into believing that the situation is real, thus making you lost in the illusion in your mind. You must take control of this by examining things from a logical and reasonable perspective. Understand that all feelings aren't reality; rather they are just responses to stimulation around us. Some intuitive people rely only on their feelings. This is where they can get into trouble. It's through the balance of mental reasoning and intuitive gut instinct that make us successful.

Addictions are hard to control. It's the body's way of responding to something that is bad for it. Your body hinders itself through the chemical and biological response to a situation or object that harms it. This is because the stimulus that the body comes into contact with has some sort of stress reducer or positive influence before it becomes harmful. Most addictive situations or substances have a very high positive reaction in the body before it becomes a negative one. The body is craving the positive stimulation, not the harmful one. We slowly become addicted to the positive enforcement of this situation and try to forget the negative side effects. The body does the same, until it is broken down. Negative spirits can trick your body to crave these substances or situations more often, breaking down your defenses more and more. You must learn to break free from addictions and find the positive stimulation from healthy situations instead. This can take time, but your body is only looking for the "high" of the situation. You must find that high in a constructive way until the body relieves itself from the negative addiction.

Tragic Moments

We're all human and living a life here in the physical world, which can be really challenging at times. Life isn't always going to be easy. For most of us in the healing and psychic community, we've probably lived harder lives than most. It's what makes us strong healers. Through certain times in our lives, very painful situations can arise: the loss of a loved one, financial difficulties, family matters, environmental tragedies, terror attacks, and so on. Through these moments, we suffer through a tremendous amount of negative energy. Fear, loss, anxiety, anger, frustration, to name a few are felt during these times. This is when you're either going to shut down completely from spirit energy or emotionally condition yourself to pull away from the negative stimulation. It's not to say that you won't feel empathy or loss during all this, but becoming emotionally stable is extremely important.

I've actually had so many things happen to me in my life since a very early age that negative situations do not affect me as much anymore. It's sort of like I've become numb to it because I've dealt with it for so long. In my life I've suffered through various situations such as cruel emotional and physical child abuse from the one person who is supposed to love you and comfort you the most, leaving me lost in a sense of true unconditional love from a parent. I've been emotionally ridiculed as a child for being overweight, people telling me how fat and unattractive I was. I've been homeless living in a van under a bridge as a teenager, then again after a divorce in my twenties. I've been through military boot camp, suffering through emotional conditioning from my commanding officers. I've suffered through financial difficulties such as losing possessions including my home and cars. I've been through a painful divorce. I've suffered through false accusations of child endangerment, tearing my heart into pieces by not being allowed to see my young children. I've suffered through back pain so severe I've had to crawl on the floor most of the day, leaving me feeling useless and vulnerable.

You name it, I've probably been through it. So why? Why would God and my guides put me through such hard times? I believe it's because I was meant to be stronger than most so that I can suffer through harder situations. They always say that what doesn't kill you, makes you stronger. I really believe this to be true. All my life my guides have been emotionally conditioning me to become a stronger person so that I can help others through their own pain and suffering. Many of you have the same situations or ones that are similar, and this is why you are drawn into this work as well. You've become stronger and more emotionally stable, which is why you are perfect for this work.

Even as strong as you are, you will still have situations that will just knock you off your feet and emotionally compromise you in every way. This is when you need to shut down mediumistically and forego any spirit rescue work until you have healed your wounds. Being emotionally unstable will not only lower your vibration, but allow for spirit or psychic attack.

Playing Into Your Fears

Spirits have an uncanny way of understanding exactly what you are afraid of and using that against you. You need to remember that spirits are energy. It's because of this that they can merge with *your* energy and go into your mind. Once they are in your mind, they can find out all sorts of details about you, such as your fears. If you're deathly afraid of spiders, then it's possible that spirits will manifest late at night as large black spiders in your room. If you're afraid of clowns, then they may manifest as a dark and spooky clown in your dreams. Spirits that are looking to harass intuitive and sensitive people will use anything against you that they feel will do the most harm. Fears are one of the best ways to do this. Once they feel that they have broken down your defenses and emotional confidence, then they move in to attach to you and feed off your energy. The best way to defend against this type of attack is to rid yourself of as many fears as you can or to understand that the fear or image they are showing you is not real and detach from any emotional compromise it may be giving you. Spirits cannot do any true harm to you if you do not allow them to. The images they are showing you aren't real. Spirits do not look like scary demons or monsters. They only manifest that way to scare you. Understand what the spirit is trying to do, and stop them in their tracks before it gets out of hand.

Understanding Fear

Fear is something that everyone will experience in their life. Whether it be through internal or external stimulus, fear is very real. Now, I know that many people out there advocate that fear is an illusion. They say that FEAR is False Evidence Appearing Real. Let me make this very clear. Fear is real. It's as real as love, because it's the opposite of love. You cannot have love without fear and vice versa. Fear is an emotion that we are born with. It's a natural response to seek security and protection that's been passed down through our normal evolution as human beings. I believe what other mediums or spiritual teachers are trying to say is that fear is very real; however, the reason why the person fears is the illusion. This I agree with. The reasons why we fear something is because we've either learned through instruction, experience, or something from a previous life brought in with us at our birth through karma.

In life we are taught through conditional beliefs that we are to fear things. Spiders, rats, snakes, ghosts, the dark, scary sounds, haunted houses, cemeteries, weapons, screaming, unpleasant facial features, and more, are all things we've been taught to believe are really scary because they will either harm us or threaten us in some way. It doesn't mean that it's true. It just means that if you've seen the same conditional response from society or the media, you will develop the same response over time.

Other situations will be through experience. You may have had a negative experience with a situation that will lead you to fear it going forward. It doesn't mean that it will happen again, it just means your brain has been trained to fear it due to pain or anxiety that was experienced during the situation. You need to have an equally positive reaction to the same stimulation to relieve the fear that was created. Quite often you need to have multiple positive reactions to the same situation to overcome the fear. For some reason the brain can remember the response of fear much stronger and longer than the reaction of love. It's the mind's way of protecting itself.

So if fear is real but the reason for the fear is not, how can we overcome this? The answer is through multiple positive reactions to the stimulation that is causing the fear to reprogram your brain. This means that you need to not only face your fears, but overcome them through trying to understand how they can become something neutral or positive. If you're afraid of heights, slowly go up higher and higher on an object and try laughing or singing when you do. If you fear bugs, try to hold one at a time and learn how important it is and how it is positively affecting the planet. If you are afraid of certain stimulation such as yelling, try yelling positive affirmations, and smile when you are doing it. Try having someone do the same thing to you and see how you feel. It's by replacing fear with love that corrects the negative thought patterns. It's funny how we let fear control our lives as much as we do. We only need to understand that our mind and our intentions can change our whole outlook in life. You have more control and power over your fears than you can imagine.

As explained before, love is the opposite of fear. By filling your mind, body, and spirit with love during a time of fear, the fear can be resolved or eliminated completely. The best way to do that, other than the ways listed above, is through positive affirmations, prayer, centering yourself, grounding your energy, or surrounding the fear with love.

Positive Affirmations

Positive affirmations are strong, loving, and comforting statements that claim that something is true. By stating positive affirmations again and again, we reset our brains to believe in these statements. Just like negative reinforcement can get you to believe in something bad about yourself, positive affirmations can change or eliminate those negative beliefs to make you feel good about yourself or situations in your life. Many people have a hard time doing this because they are so used to the negative reinforcements that have structured their complete belief system. Modern society is seemly based on these negative reinforcements. If you feel funny or uncomfortable saying something positive about yourself, then it's probably that you've been affected by negative beliefs for so long that it's hard to imagine it any other way. By affirming uplifting and inspirational thoughts, you can actually bring positive energy to yourself. Break away from the negativity.

Some of the best affirmations that I've encountered are:

Personal

- I'm a strong and beautiful person.
- I'm becoming a better person every day.
- I'm loved and cherished by the people around me.
- I'm special in every way.
- I'm good enough.
- I trust myself.
- I'm happy with who I am.
- I love myself.

Situations

- I am loved and protected.
- I can handle this.
- Things are better than I expect.

- I'm learning through this.
- I make the right choices.
- I trust my intuition and wisdom.
- I choose to see my family as a gift.
- I am loved by my friends and family.
- I can, I will, I believe in me.

Prayers

Prayers are another great way to send positive thoughts out to help eliminate fear. Prayer is our way to talk to our God and our spiritual team for love, guidance, and support. Try to take time out every day for a short prayer. Not only do prayers send out your love to spirit, but it also says that you believe they are there and you are grateful for having them in your life. Prayers are especially important when you are faced with worry, grief, sadness, anger, guilt, or any other type of fear. By connecting to God, we can relieve some of these emotions knowing that God is by our side supporting us every step of the way. My favorite prayers that help during instances of fear are:

A Prayer for Peace of Mind

God, we bless you for our lives, we give you praise for your abundant mercy and grace we receive. We thank you for your faithfulness even though we are not that faithful to you. We ask you to give us all around peace in our mind, body, soul, and spirit. We want you to heal and remove everything that is causing stress, grief, and sorrow in our lives. Please guide our path through life and make our enemies be at peace with us. Let your peace reign in our family, at our place of work, businesses, and everything we lay our hands on. Amen

The Serenity Prayer

God grant me the serenity to accept the things I cannot change; courage to change the things I can; and wisdom to know the difference. Living one day at a time; Enjoying one moment at a time; Accepting hardships as the pathway to peace; Taking, as He did, this sinful world as it is, not as I would have it; Trusting that He will make all things right if I surrender to His Will; That I may be reasonably happy in this life and supremely happy with Him Forever in the next. Amen.

Guide Me Lord

Guide me Lord, you are my heart, you are my strength, you are my hope. Teach me Lord, and guide my way I love you more each passing day.

Hold My Hand in Weakness

Lord God, you are my strength. Hold my hand in my weakness, and teach my heart to fly. With you, there's nothing to fear, nothing to worry about. Hold me tight in your embrace, so that I can be stronger than the challenges in my life. Amen.

Centering and Grounding

During times of worry or fear, you must try to remain calm and in control. It's not always going to be easy, especially when spirits seem heavy, dark, and dangerous. We have to remember during these times, spirit is showing you the best or worst they have at that moment. It's similar to an animal bearing its teeth before a fight or a bird expanding their feathers out to make themselves look larger in front of their enemy. They display their strongest and heaviest energy at first to try to convince you that they are more dominant. They do this because they understand that we are the ones who have the control, and they will do everything they can to make us believe otherwise. Once you understand that, it's all downhill from there. Remember, you have the power, they only pretend they do.

So how do we go from a place of panic and fear to a place of calmness and security? It's by grounding yourself and centering your energy. Emotions can take hold of you before you know it. Your body has a natural mechanism to fight or flight, so your body will start displaying symptoms before you even know what's happened to you. Some of the ways that your body will respond to fear are heavy breathing; fast heart rate; pounding headache; sweating; knots in your stomach; feeling like everything is in slow motion; spinning feelings; immediate anger, panic, sadness, and crying; and so on. Once you start feeling any of these symptoms, you need to use some of the below tips to start reducing or diminishing the anxiety that brought on these feelings.

Breathing

Breathing is one of the best ways to start centering your energy back to a neutral and calm state. Breathing is a way to bring a natural flow of energy back into your body. By taking a few deep breaths, you help your body gain back its natural rhythm of breathing. This helps reduce your heart rate and circulation.

Heavy, measured breathing also helps you gain control over your own thoughts. You become grounded during the heavy, slow breathing because you're allowing your mind to center onto a focused task. Regular, deep breathing also has a natural calming effect, allowing your body to relax. This is very important when faced with anxiety.

Think

Remind yourself that you are in control because this spirit is within the physical realm. Your physical life force has priority over the spirit life force residing in the physical plane. Spirits that decide to remain within the physical plane have an understanding under spiritual law that they cannot disrupt or go against the free will of a physical life force. That's not to say we have more rights than spirits do; it's just to state our priority in the physical realm due to our spiritual journey in a physical life. As a medium, clearer, or investigator who works within the spirit world, you must have a firm understanding of spiritual law.

Ground

As you center yourself with your breathing and your understanding of spiritual law, you can start focusing your attention to your energy. As you are protected from harm with your spiritual team, you are also protected and healed by the energy of Mother Earth. You are a spiritual being in a physical body. This means that you are the balance of spirit and Earth. By bringing both spirit and Earth energy into your body, you can center and balance yourself.

Start by imagining your aura expanding out and up to merge in with the white light of divine energy. Imagine this white light shining down upon you and radiating all around you to form a shield or bubble of light around your body. Allow this white light to penetrate into your energy and surround your heart chakra with white light. As you do this, imagine your root chakra, which is at the base of your tailbone, expanding and radiating a red light that shines down toward the ground. Sense and imagine this red beam of light moving down further into Mother Earth, penetrating through the Earth's crust, and slowly making its way down far into the Earth. Find a deep, thick root to wrap this red energy cord around and start bringing up the energy of Mother Earth into your root chakra. This is your anchor into Earth's energy. It will help stabilize you and ground your energy. Imagine this red cord moving up your body into your center heart chakra. Let the energy sit there and expand all around you. This red cord will now merge with the divine white light creating a soft pink color that replaces both white and red colors. This is your balance of spirit and Earth. You are now grounded and balanced. Remember to give gratitude to spirit and Earth for the loving energy they provide.

Surrounding Fear with Love

Surrounding fear with love is achieved through energy work using visualization and intention. I use this when I feel that something seems out of my control. As stated above, love is the opposite of fear. So, when you connect in with something that provokes an emotion or thought of fear, visualize love surrounding the fear to change its vibration. The best way to think about love is through a visual and emotional expression. Color associations with love are pink, rose, white, or gold. All colors have some sort of love vibration connected to them, but these colors work more within the scope of the love vibration. I like to use the color light pink.

Visually start to imagine the color of love surrounding a situation or object, encasing it within that color. While doing that, send feelings of love to it. This will automatically start changing the energy around the object. If the energy of the situation or object is not affected by it, then you might rethink being afraid of it. This is a clear indication that the situation or object comes with a high vibration and your own inner fears are creating a false perception of it. If the object or situation feels very uncomfortable in this energy, it will probably go away. If it doesn't go away quickly, continue to send it the love energy and colors until it does.

CHAPTER SIX
Where to Develop and Practice

Developing and practicing as a rescue medium is as unique as the work itself. In order to find the best choice for you, we must examine what you feel the most drawn to and comfortable working through. There are multiple outlets when developing your mediumship and rescue abilities. Some centers focus on the spiritual journey while other centers or groups concentrate more on the psychic and paranormal. There are those I strongly prefer, while others not as much, but the ultimate decision is up to you.

Psychic Centers

Psychic centers have been the most common and popular outlets for psychic and mediumship development. This would be any metaphysical store that specializes in the development of intuitive abilities, spirit communication, healing, Reiki, crystals, runes, drumming, meditation, sound therapies, crystal bowls, psychic protection, etc. These centers provide many useful lessons and practices on spiritual and psychic development. A great many of the centers have psychics and mediums that conduct readings, so think about getting a reading from a reputable psychic who can help you focus on which areas to study. Also, try to choose a good center that focuses on your growth and development. We have to remember that intuitive development is a personal journey. Everyone will have their own way of working within their unique ESP abilities. There are centers that only teach a certain way of doing things and might tell you that what you've learned from other centers is wrong, leaving you frustrated and confused. It's best to stick to a center that provides many different perspectives and teachers to help guide you on your path. Look for open-minded people. Psychic centers usually provide spirit circle development groups or mediumship training that will help you strengthen your connection to spirit. Definitely take any classes on rescue mediumship or spirit releasement as well as sit in on any indirect rescue circle groups.

Spiritualist Churches

A Spiritualist church is a church affiliated with the informal Spiritualist movement, which began in the United States in the 1840s. Spiritualist churches are now found around the world. Spiritualism is a science, philosophy, and religion of continuous life, based upon the demonstrable fact of communication, by means of mediumship, with those who live in the Spirit World. Spiritualism is a science because it investigates, analyzes, and classifies facts and manifestations demonstrated from the spirit side of existence. It is a philosophy because it studies the laws of nature, both on the seen and unseen sides of life, and bases its conclusions upon present observable facts. Spiritualism is a religion because it strives to understand and to comply with the physical, mental, and spiritual laws of nature that are the laws of God. The phenomena of Spiritualism consists of prophecy, clair abilities, laying on hands, healing, visions, trance, levitation, raps, automatic and independent writings, spirit drawings, spirit voice and materializations, psychometry, and other manifestations proving the continuity of life.

Spiritualism conducts church services, which include hands on healing, inspirational lectures, hymns, and spirit messages. Spiritual churches also conduct workshops on mediumship, healing, and other modalities in the spiritual arena. Most spiritualist churches conduct development circles that help with spirit communication. Seek out a Spiritualist church in your area if you find yourself drawn to the spiritual side of this work rather than the psychic side. Rescue mediumship was first originated from the Spiritualist churches and continues to flourish today. I believe these churches may be the best resource for you to advance your knowledge of rescue mediumship.

Build Your Own Spirit Development Circle

Finding members and building your own spirit development circle might be a good choice if there aren't any spiritual churches or psychic centers in your area. This would not be a form of development I would recommend to the untrained medium. It would be more for those of you who have studied in mediumship and psychic abilities and are ready to branch off and start your own development circle.

Learning how to protect yourself and others is vitally important, especially when you have people new to mediumship developing in your circle group. Be prepared to become a mentor or facilitator for less-educated members. Suggestions for development in your circle would be spirit protection, clearing, communication, rescue, spiritual guidance from your spirit team, meditation, grounding, healing, and spirit attachment removal.

Oftentimes development circle groups can be held at your own home—as long as you don't mind having spirits visiting. I personally do not recommend it as, for me, my home is my sacred space, and I do not let unknown spirits in. It is also not recommended if your home is occupied by those more susceptible to spirit influences, such as children or the chronically ill. I usually conduct spirit circle groups at my Spiritualist church or psychic center. You may want to consider hosting a circle group outside near a river or by the ocean as water is a wonderful conduit for healing and clearing. If you aren't able to go outside during certain times of the year, try to rent out a space that isn't too hard to maintain. Try to keep clearing tools in your space such as crystals, candles, music, incense, and other high vibrational items to cleanse after spirit communication.

Online

In today's modern world of technology there are many online resources for you to use for mediumship and rescue development. Chat groups, videos, and blogs have become easily accessible for many people. I find chat groups are great since these can connect you to people from around the world who share in your interest in the paranormal, spirit world, and rescue work. Just remember that because you are connecting with different people around the world, there will be many different views and practices on rescue work. Until recently, there hasn't been any official training or programs on rescue work, so techniques will differ. Do not let this frustrate you; try to see this as a gift. Many different perspectives are good because it allows you to try out a few styles to see what works for you. Online chat groups also provide you the chance to share your own experiences with others. You'll be amazed how many other mediums have had the same situations happen to them. For example, I've created an online chat group through Facebook called Rescue Mediumship. Please feel free to join the group to share your experiences or ask questions.

Paranormal Teams

Involvement with paranormal teams is one area I do not feel you should try to develop; rather practice and work within. Several ghost hunting teams or investigators are now working with more mediums to help the earthbound spirit once they've done their investigative work. Mediums can also help validate information that the homeowner or businessowner is experiencing. The activity known as ghost hunting has transformed into a widespread phenomena, and more investigators are opening up to spirit communication. Because of this, investigators are going to need to learn rescue work to help the spirits transition or clear spirits when they become harassing. Working as a rescue medium on these teams can be both beneficial for the paranormal investigators and earthbound spirits. Please refrain from developing your skills in this work and only include yourself on these teams once you've become more skilled and experienced.

Creating Your Own Rescue Team

Creating a team you trust is like building a family. You must work with and rely on each other as much as possible. Each one of you will not only be responsible for the protection of your own energy, but for the energy of everyone else on your team. Building a strong bond will be essential to success. I usually work with a clearer, an EVP (electronic voice phenomena) specialist, or another medium.

The majority of people will call my team when they already have an idea there is a spirit present or if they feel that they are being disturbed by spirit energy. Calls we often take are people getting harassed, scared, or hurt by spirits, and they want them removed. Other calls may be related to negative residual energy that people would like removed because it's disrupting their own energy. It may be making them feel nauseous, dizzy, confused, angry, sad, etc., which makes them very uncomfortable.

As a rescue medium, I connect with earthbound spirits so that I can communicate with them to help determine what outcome is possible at that time. There is also psychic work involved to scan the area for energy imprints and residual time placement imprints. This includes searching out to find any spiritual doors or vortexes that need to be closed.

For protection, my team's clearer will walk alongside me to help cleanse and clear while I work. She is responsible for smudging, crystal stimulation, energy stimulation, energy clearing, spirit protection work, psychic intuition, and support mediumship—all of which another rescue medium can do, but there are those who like to focus on the clearing aspect of our work and less on the spirit communication. Whichever one you feel drawn to is fine, both are equally important. My EVP specialist is more focused towards the homeowner to explain to them what we are doing and documenting anything that may come up during our work. She or he will also record the session and walk around the building asking the spirit questions. EVP specialists can additionally pick up on sounds of residual energy imprints and time placement imprints on their recorders. Mediums like to use EVP specialists when they are available, as hearing the spiritual activity helps validate the information mediums receive. It can be hard for mediums to prove what they are receiving, and the EVP work helps to confirm this information.

CHAPTER SEVEN
Psychic Protection

The field of spirit rescue can be a bit challenging due to the lower-level spirits that you will be counseling or clearing. There will be earthbound spirits that can become very emotionally compromised and may try to lash out at you through psychic or energy attacks. Spirits are comprised of energy; therefore, they attack with energy channeling through your thoughts and emotions. Because of this, you will need to learn how to protect yourself in a psychic and spiritual way to help minimize any chance of spirit attachment or attacks.

Auras

The easiest way for me to explain how spirits attack is through energy transfer. Everything has a vibrational frequency that emits energy. Objects such as trees, rocks, crystals, wood, water, or animate things like people, animals, and spirits all have a vibrational frequency. That frequency is determined by the state of the subject's awareness, thoughts, emotions, and interactions with other people, places, or things. When someone comes into contact with another object or person, the vibrational frequencies change slightly depending on the stimulus of the other object or person. This is achieved through the aura of a person or thing. An aura is a vibrational frequency of energy that surrounds a person or object. The frequency of this aura changes depending on the mental or emotional state of the person. Inanimate objects do not have a fluctuation of emotions; therefore, they have a fixed frequency and display the same aura throughout their existence until they come into contact with a non-fixed frequency like the aura of a living person.

Auras change often due to the natural change of vibrational frequency. This is displayed through colors and feelings. If the person is in a joyous and happy mood, such as while celebrating a birthday party, then the vibrational frequency of the person's aura will be bright and strong. Their aura vibration will show colors associated with their thoughts and emotions. Colors often seen include pink, orange, yellow, green, purple, or blue depending on the person. The person's aura will also carry a faster vibration due to the heightened state of positive feelings. If a person were to experience the death of a family pet and were overwhelmed by sadness and grief, the aura of the person would change to a slower and lower frequency due to the accompanying negative emotions. The person's aura color may change to dark and murky colors like dark green, brown, mustard yellow, dark blue, or gray in response to negative influences. This would cause a considerable difference in frequency in the person's aura. The incoming negative aura comes closer to the person and in turn makes the person's aura weaker, creating gaps or holes in the aura. This is when the person is vulnerable the most to spirit or psychic attack.

A person's aura is a correlation of all energies within the subject's mental and emotional bodies. Simply put, everything the person has gone through in their life creates a mental and emotional imprint in the person's aura. Your mind can hold onto a lifetime of thoughts and experiences. Even when you think you've forgotten something, it's somewhere, hidden within your subconscious, and creates an imprint on your soul's connection to the mind. These imprints on your mind create their own energy vibration and merge with your aura.

The aura field actually consists of multiple layers of energy. Each layer has a frequency of vibration associated with the connection to the person. Current situations are displayed through the outer layer of the aura, with situations from the past or forgotten situations residing deep within the aura and close to the body. The part of the aura that changes the most frequently is around the head. This is due to the continual changing thoughts the person is having. Feelings or emotions in the aura usually reside around the shoulders, chest, or stomach of the person. Terms such as heartfelt, heartwarming, and heartbroken are often attributed to this region.

So how do spirits attack through the energy of a person's aura? This is done by the direct penetration of the aura through weak points. Spirits will search out areas of weakness in a person's aura and try to manipulate the frequency, creating lower and denser vibrations, making the aura even more susceptible to attack. Once the area of the person's aura merges with the energy of the spirit, the attacks escalate by manipulating the person's emotions and thoughts.

As I've stated earlier, the imprints in the aura connected to the mind have an energy link. Think of it as a river of energy. The imprint in the aura is a flowing strip of energy that connects the mind to the aura. The spirit can use this river of energy to move into the mind of the person it is attacking. Once inside the mind, the spirit can do a lot of psychological damage.

Another way spirits can attack you through your aura is by draining you of your energy. Once they've merged in with your aura, spirits can lower the aura's vibration through negative thoughts. Creating moods including depression, sadness, anger, frustration, or spirits can make you feel extremely fatigued. Physical symptoms of spirit attack are strong headache, stomachache, anxiety, digestive upset, dizziness, and pain. This is why keeping your aura strong and protected is essential in spirit work.

So how do we keep our aura strong and protected? This is through positive energy stimulation. Thoughts and emotions pertaining to positive stimulus charge the aura, creating a strong and bright vibration. This doesn't mean that you're supposed to stay happy and positive every minute of the day. It just means to pay attention to your emotions and thoughts more often so that you'll know when your aura may be compromised. Once you start feeling or thinking in a negative way, you would then create a protective shield around yourself until your thoughts and emotions again become aligned with a more positive vibration.

Shielding

In energy work, you must master the art of visualization. This is where your mind creates and influences energy around you. Just because it isn't physical, doesn't mean it's not real. If you visualize something around you, you are condensing energy around you to mold it with the power of your mind. For example, if you imagine a ball of energy in your hand, your mind is telling the energy around you to start condensing into a ball of energy in your hand. The energy within the molecules of air, electricity, and electromagnetic static start to condense together, creating this ball of energy in your hand. Just because you do not see it, doesn't mean that it isn't there. Most energy in this world is never seen, only felt. The longer you imagine this ball of energy, the greater chance of it being created. Some energy stimulus takes longer to generate and mold than others. Those with the capability of psycho-kinesis can generate this energy manipulation or stimulation much faster and easier.

So now that you know you can change the energy around you and mold it into something beneficial, you can start by imagining or visualizing this energy into a positive shield around you.

By creating a shield around you and your aura, you must learn to imagine what color and frequency works best for you for your energies' protection. Many psychics or mediums will tell you to imagine a white light as this generates a high frequency. White light may not always be the best choice for protection. Though it is a very high vibration, spirits often get drawn to the white light around you and may feel they need to merge with your energy for comfort and guidance.

Colors associated with strength, protection, and spiritual love are violet, purple, indigo, gold, silver, pink, cream, peach, and rose, and these may work better in this situation. The best way to choose the color of your shield is through using different colors and sensing how each one makes you feel. Have your spiritual team work with you and ask them to help choose the best color that works within your energy field. For myself, I use gold, indigo, and pink. In the beginning of attempting shielding, you can use any color you wish for practice. It may take time to learn how to do a proper shield, so be patient.

In the past, other teachers have told me to just imagine a bubble of light around me to raise my vibration. It was a good concept, one in which didn't quite work for me all the time. That's mainly because while I was training I didn't fully understand how the layers of energy within a person's aura were effected. Think of it as the layers within an apple. If the core of the apple is weak and moldy, the outer layers will over time become weak as well, no matter how often you protect it and shield it. This also applies to your energy. You need to start at the core and work your way out. Your core is how you feel about yourself and others. If you feel confident about yourself and compassionate and loving toward others, your core is strong and vibrant. If your true feelings are that of greed, envy, ego, and negativity, and you feel resentment, jealousy, and anger at other people, your core is dense, weak. You cannot sustain a high vibration in the outer layer if meanwhile the inner core is low. Maintaining a positive outlook on life is needed. Believe in yourself, trust yourself. Know that you are serving a higher and loving purpose. Love other people, be compassionate and giving. All of these feelings help raise your inner core's vibration.

Once you've determined that your core is strong and at a high vibration, you can then begin to imagine the energy emanating from this core expanding out and radiating within your body. Imagine it like a bright, glowing sun inside your heart that shines a light within your whole body. Allow this golden, white light to expand even further, pushing out through your body creating a glowing energy bubble around you and your aura. Everything that may have been dense or negative has been pushed out, only allowing energy at a high vibration to remain within your body. As you imagine this bubble being created around your body, start to imagine a crust or barrier with your protection color encasing your golden white bubble. Keep imagining this until you feel that your shield is strong and secure. You now have a protective shield around you. As long as you maintain confidence in your shield, negative energy cannot penetrate through this into your aura.

Physical Psychic Protection

Even though we are secure in our energy shield of protection, it helps to use tools in the field to help support our protection and keep it strong. This is done by using physical tools with a high vibration. It's much easier to maintain a high vibration within your energy if the surrounding energy is also within a higher vibration. Such tools are found within the spiritual or metaphysical communities. I am going to refrain from going into detail about some of them because it tends to be old information passed down from generation to generation, and I do not agree with some of the reasons these objects are used. I prefer to explain why I use them for energy and vibrational reasons instead.

Crystals

Crystals are great for use in energy work. They send out their own special frequency depending on the type of crystal you use. The frequency of the crystal changes as it merges in with your aura, so it's best to "feel' the energy of the crystal when buying one. I do not recommend buying them online as this doesn't give you the chance to sense if its frequency is right for you. Once you obtain your crystals, I recommend keeping at least one crystal on you most of the time. You will want to remove the crystal every now and then to cleanse. I personally recommend a high vibration crystal to wear, and grounding or cleansing crystals to have around your home just to keep your vibration high. I'm not going into too much detail about crystals since it could be a whole book in itself. The best way to think about crystals is that the darker the crystal, the more absorbing and grounding it is, the lighter the crystal, the better shielding and higher vibration it has. The choice is yours when choosing crystals. Your healers, warriors, guides, and angels will all work with you to determine which ones are right for you. To cleanse crystals, wash the crystal in salt water and soap. Then rinse the crystal with cold running water, and place it in the window ledge so that direct sunlight can dry it off. Keep it in the window for at least three days so that the sun and moon can help recharge the crystal. If grounding is needed for clearing and protection crystals, after cleaning it, burry it in the earth for three days in clean soil. Remove the crystal from the dirt and wash under cool running water. Place in the window ledge for another three days to charge.

Salt

Salt is great because it acts as a neutralizer for energy. It doesn't promote a higher vibration, rather it helps keep out negative energy from your space. There are many people who believe that sprinkling salt in the windows and doorways will help keep evil spirits at bay. I find it works for two reasons. First, it sets your thought and intent. If you put salt out and state a prayer or affirmation while doing so, you put that energy into the salt which helps maintain your intent even after you walk away. Second, it neutralizes the energy that is around that space, making the negative energy dissipate. Just remember, salt is corrosive, so putting it out on wood or metal isn't recommended. Try to put it in a small secure container instead. Sprinkling it on the ground outside can also kill grass or any plants, so try to use very little if possible.

Because salt is used so effectively in dissipating negative energy, many people use it as barriers in their homes, as a shield. Sprinkling the salt in a circle formation is very popular to help seal in the energy of the home and to block all negative energy outside the circle. Just remember that when you use salt to shield energy from coming in, you also prevent negative energy from leaving as well, trapping it inside. Make sure that all negative energy is cleared from your home before you create your salt circle.

Smudging or Incense

Smudging has been very popular in the metaphysical community. Just like salt, it helps neutralize energy. Smudging or incense is used more often because you can control the flow of energy to certain parts of your home. I recommend using incense because you can light this on a table and leave it for a while, allowing it to cleanse the area. You don't have to keep an eye on it every minute. It's a no-brainer to help cleanse your space, plus incense comes in many different fragrances, which makes your home or space smell great. If you use sage or other dried herbs for smudging, use a heat resistant bowl or object to burn it in. Walk around the space, fanning the smoke into different areas you feel are dense or in need of cleansing. Prayers and affirmations are great to use at this time as well. It sets your thought and intent into the smoke, sending it out into the atmosphere. Always extinguish the embers and never leave burning smudging supplies unattended in a room for safety.

Sounds

High vibrational sounds are great to aid in maintaining positive energy around you. Chimes, bells, crystal bowls, music, and singing are all great ways to control the energy in your space. High vibration tones help raise the energy creating a better atmosphere for positivity. I like to have music on all the time. It helps me to focus my attention on something positive, especially when the kids are running around and yelling. There are many online resources that have free high vibrational music. Keep it running in the background. It can really help change the energy of any space.

Psychic and Energy Weapons

Another form of psychic protection is through learning how to defend your own energy and people around you through protective defensive weapons. These energy weapons aren't used to attack spirits, rather they are used in self-defense when you are being attacked psychically. All energy tools will be used through visualization in your mind. Spirits come through to us mostly in our minds through various ways. Usually when you are thinking about something or when you are dreaming, spirits will invade your space and try to manipulate your energy. You'll know that a lower-level spirit is starting to invade your thoughts when you feel an intense sensation of dense, heavy, and dark energy that is approaching you. We have to remember that some of these energies are earthbound spirits that have lost their way and lash out to attack people out of anger or frustration. That isn't to say that we need to put up with it; it just means that we need to come from a place of understanding and compassion when defending ourselves.

The first thing to be made clear is that you should never use these weapons out of anger. These are very high spiritual weapons that have been gifted to us for self-defense. If you don't use them correctly, they can be taken away by your spiritual team. Second, you will be gifted each weapon at different times of your development if your spiritual team believes that you will be working more in clearing and security. Some rescue mediums never deal with such lower spirits and only work with lost, confused, or scared spirits looking to find their way. These spirits do not attack or harm, so those mediums will never need the use of these spiritual weapons. For those of you who work more as clearers of spirits, spirit attachments, lower-level entities, elementals, and other lower dimensional beings, then you will most likely use some of these weapons. Third, you should always call in your protectors and warriors when using these weapons to help you. Archangel Michael's energy is one of the best to use. Your protectors will all have their own unique energy and skill, so it's best to call them in for extra protection. Your guides will also help you learn how to use your weapons when you mediate, go on a spiritual journey, and/or they may use your dreams as a grounds for practicing your form and technique for each weapon. Don't be surprised if your guides provide lessons during these times of training. This would mean lessons from actual experiences of spirit attack. Your guides may take a step back and allow you to be compromised by a lower-level spirit. You're only going to become stronger through this work in the spirit world. It may seem hard at first. Know that you're always protected, so ask for extra assistance if you feel overwhelmed.

Sword of St. Michael

The sword of St. Michael is also known as the sword of truth and justice. It is used in defense of dark spirits that challenge the love and truth of God and all things from God. This sword may be presented to you when you are in need of very strong protection. I only use this sword for very low spiritual entities. Think of it as the most powerful weapon you have. Only use it when truly needed. This should never be misused or compromised in any way. The sword of St. Michael may show itself as a blade with a golden handle and a diamond in the middle, or it may present itself to you with no gems in the middle with just a golden handle. It all depends on what feels right for you. Those who use this sword in a battle may want to use the prayer of St. Michael before using it.

PRAYER TO SAINT MICHAEL THE ARCHANGEL

St. Michael the Archangel,
Defend us in battle.
Be our defense against the wickedness and snares of the Devil.
May God rebuke him, we humbly pray,
and do thou, O Prince of the heavenly hosts,
by the power of God, thrust into hell Satan, and all the evil spirits who prowl about the world
seeking the ruin of souls. Amen

The Shield

The shield should be presented to everyone who works with lower-level spirits. This is to be used as reflective energy. It not only shields you from energy the lower-level spirits are sending to you, but it also reflects the energy back to the sender. The shield should be presented to you in either silver or gold with wings, cross, or sword in the middle. It should be fairly light to use and carry. Ask for guidance from your guides on proper blocking techniques.

The Blades

The blades come as a pair, one for each hand. They are smaller in size so that they are easily used to move around with. These blades should come through as silver or gold with a suede band around the handle. You will probably receive holsters for your blades at the same time. Your guides will help you learn how to use them to defend and attack. As stated above, the sword and shield are not used for attacking, but these blades are. The attack maneuver is to help break up dense, negative imprints. Do not think you are hurting these energies when you are using them, rather you are weakening their energy so that they will go away.

The White Staff

This staff is not to be confused with the staff some of your guides use. This staff is made for energy protection. The staff is glowing white, standing about six feet tall. It should not have any medallion, feathers, or crystals attached. It should be received plain from your guides. The white staff glows with the light of the "divine will" to banish all negativity in your path. It should be used for protection and as a show of force and wisdom. The white staff is a symbol of divine guidance from God. It serves as a symbol that all energy is equal in the eyes of God. One form of energy shall not have control over another.

The White Whip

The white whip should be used just like the white staff, but is used more often if you should want to keep your distance from these spirits. It should be presented to you as a glowing white whip about ten feet long, with a brown, leather handle. You may feel a bit like Indiana Jones in one of his movies, but I promise you will need to learn how to use it when you feel threatened. The white whip carries a very high vibration that shocks or stuns the spirit.

Sending Out White Light

Sending out white light is not a physical weapon to use as this energy comes from within you. It still is used in defense and helps to weaken negative spirits while they are attacking. Imagine white light emanating from your hands. The glowing white light can be used to form a cluster of energy that you throw out to the spirit. Imagine white light balls of energy thrusting out of your hand, shooting out across the room into the vibration of the spirit. This can weaken the spirit, causing them to retreat. Again the white light is a high vibration that the dense, negative spirit feels uncomfortable around. Another way to use the white light is to imagine the white light shining out of your hand like a strobe light. When doing this, imagine this strobe light effect entering the energy of the spirit. The fast and high vibration of this energy can weaken the negative spirit, sending it away.

CHAPTER EIGHT

Residual Energy vs. Spirit Energy

One of the most challenging tasks in rescue and clearing work is being able to tell the difference between spirit energy and residual energy. Not only are you going to need to know the difference, but you're also going to need to know how to handle both forms of energy. So, learning the many variations of energy and vibrational levels is going to really help you along with your training and work in rescue and clearing. Residual energy is just what it sounds like. It's energy that is left behind after an event that has left its "mark" or imprint. Residual imprints can be made in many different ways and can show themselves to you in various forms. But before I go into too much detail, let's first explain a little bit about why energy is left behind.

How Residual Energy Forms

All matter contains an energy vibration. As we explained before about auras, this energy is either fixed or changeable depending on whether this is a living or non-living element. Earth, air, fire, and water are all elements that hold their own unique energy vibration. When it comes into contact with another form of energy that is not of its own vibration, the energy signature of the matter changes. Depending on the strength and force of the situation, it can either dissipate very quickly and change back to the original energy signature, or it can hold onto the new energy form for some time.

For example, tree "A" carries its own unique vibration because of where it is located in the world, what leaves it has, where it is planted, and what may or may not be planted next to it. If a new tree "B" were to be planted right next to it, the vibration of the tree would change to reflect the new energy surrounding it. If the new tree "B" is removed, then the tree "A" would return to the vibration it originally began with before the new tree "B" arrived. That's how energy works. It transfers, blends, and enhances when it comes into contact with other forms of energy. Now if the new tree "B" were to fall onto tree "A" and the fall of this tree was intense enough to do some damage, the original vibration of tree "A" would change to reflect this new energy. This new energy of the tree "A" would stay constant for a long time because the new energy was so forceful that it changed the original energy signature. This new energy would remain even if the new tree "B" was removed. Why? Because the residual energy from the forceful fall would remain as a layer of new energy on the tree "A," changing the tree's constant energy vibration to a new one.

Everything we do sends out a stream of energy to the surrounding people or objects around us. Each object around us can absorb our energy vibration once it comes into contact with our aura. Depending on how the object reacts to the new vibration, determines how long our energy is absorbed into it.

Denser and lower vibrations usually "stick" around much longer than lighter and higher vibrations. This is because of the structure and intensity of the energy. For example, if you were to have a room filled with people celebrating the birth of a new baby, the energy of the room would become light and bright. This energy would dissipate very quickly. If a room was filled with people grieving over the death of a loved one, the energy of the room would be heavy and dark. This energy would take much longer to dissipate due to its heavier vibrational frequency. Think of heavy energy like mud or glue. It can stick very easily and feel very dense and restricting. Often people will say that the energy is so thick, you can cut it with a knife. That isn't too far from the truth. The denser the vibration, the better chance of it manifesting into a more semi-physical form.

Depending on the placement of residual imprints, you may get different reactions. Places in the world that have certain metals, rocks, or environmental structures can act like sponges for residual energy. These elements can retain energy much longer than others, which is why residual imprints remain longer in some areas. In some cases, the residual imprint may never dissipate depending on the strength of the sponge effect or how much residual energy is left behind.

Residual imprints can also overlap each other like layers. This can happen over time when the area is old and still has a lot of activity. The residual imprints that are the oldest are at the bottom with most recent imprints layered at the top. Due to the number of layers in a residual imprint, the energy becomes denser, making it harder to dissipate. Every time someone comes into an area with a lot of residual energy, the person can add residual imprints if they experience heavy emotions such as fear, anxiety, or excitement. It's called feeding the residual imprint. A place may seem haunted for many, many years even when the earthbound spirit has left, due to the building of the residual energy.

Time Placement Imprint

Learning how to read the energy imprint of the residual mark is extremely important. This can explain what happened, why the residual mark was left, and most importantly, that it's not an intelligent spirit (ghost). When you learn how to read the residual imprint, you may notice events being played over and over again. This is a time placement residual imprint. This is when some dense energy may repeat itself until it is cleared or dissipated away. Think of it like a rerun of a show being played over and over again. These time placement imprints usually occur when the event happened over a length of time and the whole situation was recorded in the imprint.

One of the most common reasons why spirit energy is confused with residual energy is because many spirits can easily hide in a time placement residual imprint, especially if the time placement imprint was created at the time of their death. The spirit remains in the event, which gets played over and over again because their mental and emotional state is fixed in that moment of time. By clearing away residual time placement imprints, you can help the spirit's perceived reality change, making them more receptive to help.

Different Forms of Residual Energy

Residual energy may take on many forms. It all depends on the strength and situation of the event that determines what form is left. Forms of residual imprints can be found through sound, taste, smell, feeling, or image.

Sound: Residual energy that carries the vibrational frequency of sound usually occurs because the imprint of the noise was significant enough to get "trapped" in the imprint. Noises of footsteps, gun shots, storms, slammed doors, or car crashes can be left behind. If someone died suddenly in their house by falling down the stairs, you may hear the residual time placement of the fall on the stairs because the impact left a mark where it happened. It doesn't mean that the spirit is still in the house; it just means the imprint is heavy enough to manifest, usually through auditory means.

Taste or smell: Tastes and smells can be left behind in residual energy depending on its importance. Oftentimes the smells of gunpowder, smoke, fire, rain, or dampness can all leave their mark in the imprint, as well as tastes of food, blood, or dirt can be left in the mark. If you were to walk through the field of a historically known battleground, the residual imprint smell of the gunpowder or the residual taste of sweat or blood might be experienced. It's a good idea to pay attention to the smell and taste as it can help determine what was happening at the time of the event. All marks in the imprint will be beneficial in telling its story.

Feelings: The most common type of residual imprint is a feeling or emotion. Emotions carry very intense vibrations that can lead to the creation of the residual imprint. Feelings or emotions such as fear, loss, anger, pain, jealousy, and so on, will leave a heavy residual mark. Every time you come into contact with this energy imprint, you take a chance of experiencing all the feelings of the people involved in the creation of the imprint. This in turn can be very overwhelming for the medium. It's best to understand that these feelings are not your own, and you must shield yourself from negative influences.

Image: Physical forms can be left behind as well. Human forms, animals, or objects can be left in a residual mark depending on its importance in the event. If an animal was killed by a passing car and the crash was very strong and forceful, the imprint of the animal's body would be left behind. A good example would be the "handprint"' analogy I explained in my first book, *Toward the Light*. If you smack your hand down on a table, it will leave an energy image of your handprint there for some time until it dissipates. In a way, this can be demonstrated with modern thermal imaging as heat and energy from your hand is passed on to the table appearing as a temporary heat imprint. The same situation can occur with the imprint of the animal. The image of the animal will stay fixed in the energy of the ground or surrounding area until the residual energy of the animal dissipates.

Telling the Difference

Now that you understand how residual energy works, you can begin to determine if the energy you are picking up on is residual or spirit. Since we understand that residual marks can manifest to appear identical to spirit, such as apparitions, sounds, and feelings, we need to connect in with the energy to determine if the energy has any intelligence to it. I've listed a handful of ways here that have worked for me and other mediums in the field. They are commonly referred to as "clair" abilities to make it easier to understand what might work best for you depending on your strengths.

Clairvoyance

Those with the strength of clairvoyance will rely heavily on the ability to see energy. Residual time placements will be easy to see, which will help you understand what took place in that area. These residual marks will appear different than spirits because they have different layers of energy around them. Spirits will still have an aura around them that may hold many colors around them depending on their mood or mental status. Their auras are constantly changing, just like we are here in the physical world. There are auras that will shine brightly while other auras will show as muddy and dark. In contrast, residual imprints usually have a fixed aura around them because it stays fixed in the moment of its creation.

Clairaudience

Mediums with clairaudience rely heavily on the ability to hear the energy around them. When spirits connect in with mediums gifted with this ability the sound of the spirit is usually heard through the inner psychic ear. It's like hearing the voice of the spirit directly in your mind. When a medium connects in with a residual imprint, the sound is usually heard from the outer ear, like a physical sound.

Clairsentience

Mediums with the ability to feel the energy of residual marks and spirits will rely heavily on their reaction to the energy. This also means that you have the ability to sense and feel how the energy reacts to you when you enter the room. Energy that manifests from residual marks does not have an intelligence attached to it. Marks will only manifest the form of residual energy. The energy will not react to you through intelligent stimulation, such as trying to initiate a conversation. I like to think of this as the echo effect. It's like sending your energy out to see if there is a response. If the energy responds to you by sending energy back to you, then you know it's spirit energy. If there is no response, then it's residual energy. The aura of the residual imprint may change, but this is only because your aura is connecting into it, changing its vibration. Simply put, the energy of the residual imprint will not respond to your stimulation.

Not all of the techniques I've mentioned will be successful for you. You may have to discover your own way of determining the source of the energy you encounter. Once you do understand what works best for you, use it to your full advantage. Knowledge of the differences between residual imprints and spirit energy will change your focus during your work. It may also save you time at the site if you know you only need to clear residual energies instead of completing a rescue.

CHAPTER NINE
Spiritual Doors and Vortexes

As we dig deeper down the rabbit hole of spiritual and psychic development, we start to form an understanding that we are surrounded by many forms of energy, whether it be physical, spiritual, paranormal, universal, or elemental. Each form of energy carries its own distinctive vibration that allows it to reside within a level of energy supporting it. The Earth has an energy barrier that has many layers within itself. Within each layer of energy, there are cracks or holes that allow this energy to flow from one level or layer to another. These layers of energy in the Earth's field also connect to layers of energy within the spiritual and universal fields of energy, wherein lie many cracks or holes to allow energy to flow between as well. The psychic or metaphysical community would call these holes spiritual doors or portals. It's most common for those with ESP abilities to sense and feel these doors when they come into contact with them. The strong pulse of energy that resonates from these doors is enough to draw in those with extra sensory abilities to study and learn from them. No one exactly knows what lies on the other side of these spiritual doors since only non-physical energy can transfer through them. We can only know what may come through the door depending on where the door is, what the vibration is like, and the intent of the door.

Spiritual Doors

Spiritual doors will be felt differently through various means. Each medium will have their own distinctive way of sensing a spiritual door based on their strengths. Most spiritual doors or portals are felt through physical and non-physical means. Those with ESP abilities will sense the non-physical energy associated with the spiritual doors better than those without ESP abilities.

Non-Physical Signs of Spiritual Doors

Psychic Visions of Spiritual Doors

Colors that manifest from these doors can show themselves on "our side" of the door, alerting us to an open pathway to another realm. Colors associated with the layer of energy it comes from will move through the door, pushing its way into space on the other side. Spiritual doors may have colors like emerald green, turquoise, purple, indigo, electric blue, and white, and will be seen by those with clairvoyance abilities. Visual apparitions of doors can be seen as columns of energy or a hole in the floor where the energy is coming up through. Swirling colors around these columns of energy can be seen, which may radiate from these doors into the room. Doors that carry a dense vibration might distort the energy of the room, creating a shadow in an area of the room. That area may seem darker than the rest of the room, as if the light was removed from that space

Sensing or Feeling the Energy

Those with ESP abilities may sense feelings of a strong pulse of energy or a vacuum-like effect from the door. The feelings of being drawn in or pushed out depends on which way the energy is moving. If the spiritual door opens to allow energy to move into our area, you will feel a strong flow of energy being pushed out. If a spiritual door opens to retract the energy that brought it, it will feel like energy is being pulled in. The energy flow can be changed by thought and intent. Dark and dense spiritual doors can give you a sense of being watched as if something is sensing you from the other side of the door. These spiritual doors have a very different vibration from what is in the room, so sensing them isn't difficult.

Physical Senses from Spiritual Doors

Visual

Bright lights or "spots" in the room can indicate angelic energy coming through a high vibrational spiritual door. The bright light is an indication of the light seen from the other side when the door quickly opens. Spirits from the other side can also use these doors, so seeing them in a room may indicate you are being visited by loved ones.

Dizziness

A spinning-like feeling or episode of dizziness can be sensed if you walk through a door. It's usually due to the change of frequency and the body senses the change of pressure. The pressure can affect the inner ear, which may cause vertigo. Quite often this feeling goes away quickly once you walk out of the door.

Stomach Sensations

Feelings of queasiness or pressure in the stomach are felt due to your solar plexus chakra picking up on the change of energy. Our solar plexus controls our clairsentient ability, which is the sense of feeling. The solar plexus chakra may get over-stimulated, which may cause pressure, upset, or nausea when sensing a spiritual door.

Sounds

All manner of sounds can project from spiritual doors. Higher vibration doors can have sounds like bells, chimes, musical notes, or sounds we can't even describe on Earth. They are usually very loving and comforting when you hear them, like you know you are being cared for and watched over. Doors with a lower vibration usually have sounds that are hard to hear. The lower and denser sound vibrations are not usually sensed by our ears unless you are familiar with them. Cracking noises, deep thumping, or tones with low octaves can be heard. Whistling noises can sometimes be heard outside if the door is extracting energy into the door.

Vortexes

One of the most common ways to see spiritual doors through our ESP abilities is through the spiral energy flow that forms when multiple energy vibrations merge together. This is what we call a vortex. Just like a tornado emerges from a storm when two or more pressure systems merge together, a vortex will be created when low pressure and high pressure merge together.

So what is the difference between vortexes and spiritual doors? This is easy, as spiritual doors are the opening space for energy to flow, while a vortex *is* the energy flow. The best way to think of the difference is to think about it like a subway tunnel. The tunnel is like a spiritual door, open and ready even if a train is not going through. Once the train goes through, it still remains open and ready. It doesn't cease to exist unless someone closes down the subway or demolishes it. The same rules apply for spiritual doors. A vortex gets created when the train moves through the tunnel, down the subway toward its destination. In other words, the vortex gets created when energy flows in a direction that merges two different vibrations together and ceases to exist when the energy flow stops. Not all of them create vortexes. We don't know exactly why some do and some don't, but we have a feeling it has something to do with intent of the door and the force of the energy flow.

Not All Vortexes are Spiritual Doors

When spiritual practitioners or energy healers open spiritual doors to transmute energy, they can sometimes create a vacuum-like effect that creates a vortex. This allows the energy to flow in the direction of its destination to be received by spiritual help in other planes or realms. So, in a sense, they aren't trying to create a door, rather a flow of energy that carries away from the person being healed. Once the transfer of energy is complete, the vortex closes and the constant energy vibration stabilizes itself. Vortexes can be created even when spiritual energies are not involved. This is when two vibrations move together to enhance the flow of energy. People transfer energy all the time without realizing it and can create a vortex of energy that flows from one person to another. These are very small vortexes and can't always get noticed unless you are a strong clairsentient.

Vortexes can also be created when two or more strong energies merge together like lay lines. When two or more lay lines cross over each other, their energies create a vortex. There are a few places in the world, like one in Sedona, Arizona, or one at Stonehenge, that have a vortex due to this merger of energy. Vortex energy occurs most commonly through lower pressure or dense energy, pushing up into a neutral or higher vibration around it. That is why vortexes can be sensed often at places where high electromagnetic energy fields collide together.

Places Where Spiritual Doors Might Form

Spiritual doors are more common than you think and the number of doors in an area depends on the electromagnetic energy, spiritual energy, and metaphysical practices of the area. There are common places that spiritual doors can be found. Higher spiritual doors that allow spiritual helpers to serve in a loving, comforting, and supporting role are:

- Churches
- Hospitals
- Schools

- Military stations
- Sacred spiritual retreats or camps
- Places of historical significance
- Places of prayer or vigil
- Battlegrounds
- Areas of high numbers of casualties

Elemental energy helps with the energy of the planet. Elementals can create spiritual doors when they travel in and out of the physical planes' vibration to be of service. Places that have spiritual doors that allow denser vibrations that serve to protect, heal, or support the Earth through elemental energy are:

- Areas impacted by ecological disasters
- Areas that are damaged by destructive weather conditions
- Areas of high concentration of damaging chemicals or toxic waste
- Volcanic areas
- Forests with old-growth trees
- Rivers, lakes, or oceans
- Gardens
- Deserts
- Mountains
- Areas of tectonic activity
- Areas where lay lines meet

Lower vibration doors that allow negative entities to move in and out can be formed either through the intent of the entity or through our intent. All it takes is a shift from one vibration to another quickly that creates that crack or split in the layers that allows these spiritual doors to open. Activities that allow these doors to open are:

- Playing paranormal-based games that invoke the spirits or demons
- Spiritual rituals that call to lower-level entities
- Demonic chanting
- Talking about demonic energy for prolonged periods of time
- Rituals with intent on harming others or yourself
- Prolonged sexual or physical abuse of others or yourself
- Bringing in demonic energy from objects moved into a space
- Abuse of spiritual practices or psychic arts

Spiritual Doors in Mirrors

There have been countless stories of people who claim that mirrors have allowed spirits to wander in and out of their house because of the spiritual door that resides inside the mirror. These people honestly believe that these mirrors are doorways to the spiritual and paranormal realm because they've experienced the doorway themselves through paranormal occurrences. For those in the non-spiritual community, it's hard to believe that a mirror made of glass can create spiritual doors. Why would a mirror create or hold a spiritual door more often than other objects in your home? Is this something made up and folklore, or is there a real explanation behind these occurrences? The answer lies in what you believe. For myself, I've experienced many situations through mirrors with spirits, demons, projections, and doorways that were hard to believe at first, but the knowledge my guides and spiritual teachers gave me made sense of it all.

My teachers explained to me the reason why a mirror can become a spiritual door is because of its reflection. A reflection is an opposite projection of the image it is facing. In this reflection our universe here in the physical world is reflected into the mirror, creating its own universe within that environment. This new universe or environment now carries a vibration created by the reflection. In that new vibration, spiritual realms and doors can be created as well.

Circumstances that have a negative vibration usually have the most impact on these mirrors. That's because the mirror is still a physical object, which carries a denser vibration than spiritual energies. Spiritual beings with lower vibrations can attach to these mirrors, reside in the reflected environment, and create a door for other spirits to move through as well. This might explain why more negative spiritual experiences occur than positive ones through mirrors.

Don't get too overwhelmed and panic about all the mirrors in your home. Most mirrors do not hold spiritual doors or spirits within them. This is on rare occasions that usually result after spiritual, paranormal, demonic practices, or any other ritualistic experience. Spirits that get drawn into the home or building need a place to hide or escape so that they are undetected. They can do this through the reflection of the mirror. While in the mirror, they can change the vibration of the mirror, which creates a door or portal to allow other entities to come through. That is why many people cover their mirrors before performing any spiritual rituals or ceremonies.

Closing Spiritual Doors

Now that we know how to sense these spiritual doors, we have to decide if having them around is in our best interest. Lighter and brighter spiritual doors are around all the time, usually without our even sensing them. They usually open up when spirits make their transition or when angelic energy, healing energy, or protection energy is coming through to be of assistance. These might be guides, mentors, or ancestors to help you, so it's best to allow them in your space for your own benefit.

Spiritual doors with lower vibrations can be either through elemental energy, earthbound spirit energy, entities from other realms, or non-human negative entities (demonic). We can't assume that just because the vibration is heavy and dense, that it doesn't serve a positive purpose. Elemental energy can be very dense because they carry the vibration of the Earth. Depending on the level of energy they reside in, the denseness can be very powerful and strong. This strength can be used for healing, grounding, protecting, and reconstructing of energy. The place that houses this spiritual door may be in need of heavy elemental healing due to hazardous conditions. It's not our place to determine if it's needed or not, especially if the area does not belong to us. Usually this energy will feel comforting, nurturing, or creative depending on the work it is doing. People are so busy running from the dark, they don't realize that it has its own special purpose in this work. Light energy can't fix everything. There must be a union between the light and the dark so that all energy sources within our universe can be supported. The universe seeks a natural balance.

Energy from a door that feels threatening would be one to close. The threatening feeling indicates that the intention from this door is not beneficial for you or your space. Lower-level negative entities can use these doors to move in and out of areas to harass those in our physical world. Lower-level entities or entities from other realms can use our bodies as hosts due to the lower physical vibration our bodies have. Our higher spiritual bodies are affected when entities merge with our physical bodies. These lower-level entities would not be able to effect higher spiritual beings as they carry too high of a vibration that make the negative entities uncomfortable. That's why they are so interested in us here in the physical world. We are so fascinating to them; they can't help but take over our bodies to learn more about us.

These lower-level beings aren't always looking to attach to us through these doors, sometimes they only wish to view and observe us. Regardless of the reason why they make the doors, it's best to try to close them when you can. This can be done just like any other energy work through visualization and energy stimulation.

Quite often I will sense spiritual doors when I do my "walkthrough" of a place that has a disturbance. I can sense these spiritual doors open by their vibration and get a feel for the intention of the door. If the intention is negative, I begin to close the door through visualization. For me, I feel and see spiritual doors. Each door can look different depending on its purpose, but for the most part they look like columns or vertical beams of energy moving from the ground upward into the room.

If you do not see a spiritual door, but rather feel it, you can still do this visualization if you imagine this feeling to be a beam of energy or an energy cluster.

Visualization

Start by imagining the dense energy as a beam of energy moving up from the floor. Remember to shield yourself and ground yourself into Mother Earth for protection. Ask for the help from your guides, angels, and protectors in the spirit world. Use the steps that follow as a guide.

We have to change the energy vibration of the door to close it and push it back down, out of the room.

1. Put up your hands and face them toward the spiritual door; start pushing higher and lighter energy into the door.
2. Imagine this door condensing and closing. The beam of energy will become like a thin line of energy moving upward from the ground.
3. Put your hands on the top of this thin beam and start pushing it down into the ground. You're not pushing it into the Earth energy, rather you are pushing it back within itself.
4. Once the beam is gone and you see or feel a dense hole in the floor from the spiritual door, imagine the hole condensing even further and closing.
5. Visualize an "X" over the space to dissipate the energy and manifest a lock over the space.
6. Ask for protective elemental and spiritual energy to stand over the door until it completely dissipates; this could take a few days.

There will still be residual energy in the room left over from the energy that escaped the spiritual door. This is where you would need to cleanse and clear all residual energy from the home. This is what I call "cleaning house." Removal of all residual energy is explained in the next chapter.

CHAPTER TEN
Energy Clearing

Energy clearing is really just like it sounds. It's clearing, removing, or changing the energy signature in your home. Everyone has some form of residual energy in their home, business, or place of service. Anytime you have activity in a space, you have the chance of forming residual energy imprints or clusters. These imprints or clusters can build and become stronger every time you add energy to it. Usually, the same vibration of energy clusters together due to "like energy attracts like energy." So, every time you have a situation that leaves a residual mark, it can cluster with energy already in the room, forming an even stronger residual imprint. These imprints can start affecting your emotional well-being or health over time depending on how strong the imprint is.

As we learned in the chapter on residual energy, people can sometimes mistake residual imprints as spiritual energy and call in help to remove this energy from their home. This is when you would start assessing the space by doing a "walkthrough" of the area.

The Walkthrough

Before you even go into a home or a place of interest, you would want to walk around the building to get a sense of what might be going on outside. Pay attention to the feel of the area.

- Are there elementals in the yard?
- Are there a lot of rocks, metals, or structural details that may hold residual energy like a sponge?
- Are there old or historical areas nearby?
- Is this an area that once was a resting place or cemetery?
- Are there any environmental disturbances or situations that can be effecting the energy of the surrounding area?

These would be things to check out first before assessing the inside of the building. It will all help determine what might be going on inside. Once you make the decision to move inside, always bring your shield up, ask for protection, and call in your spiritual team. Even if there isn't any spirit activity in the home, you can still come into contact with heavy residual energy, entities that manifest from these imprints, or spiritual doors that might have opened. You never know what you're going to walk into, so it's best to stay protected at all times.

There are steps that I take during my walkthrough that help make things run faster and smoother. You don't have to follow these steps, but I recommend using them if you haven't come up with your own system of energy clearing.

Assessing the Situation

- Walk around the home or space and "feel out" the energy. Are there clusters of energy that feel different from the rest of the space?
- When you come into contact with an energy imprint, read into it, and sense what it might be. Is it a door? Is it a cluster of residual emotions or a situation? Is it an entity?
- When you walk through and read energy, you can often pick up on historical imprints. You might get visual images of what the space might have looked like before there were any changes to the area. This is all picked up on the residual imprint of the original structure.
- Get a feel for what might be going on in the space. Is there a lot of tension, fear, or abuse going on in the physical world, namely the current occupants, that might be bringing in negative imprints?

Clearing the Energy

Negative Forces

Always clear away or dissipate negative entities first. Most of these entities are not demons, rather they are created from the dense, heavy residual clusters that form into its own being. I'll discuss this in detail later in the negative entities chapter as well as how to dissipate their energy.

Doors

Close all suspect spiritual doors. These doors can let in other entities or other beings that will continue to manifest during your energy clearing. So why not close them before clearing entities? Entities can create doors, too. So, unless you clear the entities first, they will continue to open many new doors to make it difficult for you. For some reason I found it took longer for doors to let in energy than it did for entities to create doors. It all has to do with timing. If possible, have someone work on the spiritual doors while you dissipate the entity (if there is one).

Clean and Clear

Work on clearing all leftover residual energy from the space through use of energy clearing techniques and tools.

Prayers and Intentions

Recite prayers and affirmations to complete the energy change, and ask for protectors to help maintain a neutral or positive vibration.

Clearing Techniques

In spirit rescue, people clear energy differently, and I find that it really doesn't matter how it's done; it only matters that it's done right. When I do my clearing work, I use three techniques that help maximize the efficiency of the clearing and help shield the home so that the energy does not return. These three techniques of clearing energy imprints and clusters are:

1. Energy manipulation through visualization.
2. Tools that clear and shield against negative energy.
3. Calling in spiritual helpers to transmute energy or store it for better use somewhere else.

Energy Manipulation

Energy can be manipulated or changed either through spirit, tools, or through you. When you connect in with a residual imprint that needs to be cleared, you can either use tools to help change the vibration of the area, or you can push out the energy through visualization techniques. I use both. I first use visualization techniques to clear energy away; then I work on the residual energy roaming or lingering around the house after with tools.

Visualization can be done any way that you find dissipates the energy or clears it away. I like to imagine pushing the energy out of the house through windows. From there, the angels that work with me take the energy and either transmute it or send it where it can be the most beneficial in the universe. If I didn't do that, the energy would just come right back in once I left. Some clearers create and use vortexes to transmute the energy out. I personally like to use spirtual guides, but do what feels right for you.

Visualization Steps to Clear Residual Energy

1. Visualize the residual energy as a big ball of energy. It appears dense and dark.
2. Imagine white light or positive energy from your hands radiating out toward this dense residual energy.
3. Visualize the white light from your hands pushing the heavy, dense residual energy out of the home. You must go slow because it takes time for the positive energy in your hands to change and stimulate the energy in the cluster.
4. Remember to put your tools we've covered in the previous chapters to use. Smudging, crystals, salt, music, and singing bowls/bells all are powerful tools to supplement your abilities in clearing a space.

Spiritual Helpers

Working with certain spiritual helpers is going to be more of a personal preference. There are mediums who only work with angels, there are mediums who work with cosmic beings, and there are clearers who work with elemental energy, so it really depends on where you feel the most connected. For me, I tend to work with clearing guides, angels, elementals, or ancient energy from Mother Earth.

Clearing Guides: While getting to know your spiritual team, you're going to connect with guides that will help you with transmuting energy or clearing energy from locations. These guides are strong light beings that specialize in energy creation and stimulation. The guides are very wise and powerful ancient beings that have a deep sense of knowing where and when to send energy for the betterment of the universal energies. I always trust that they know best when clearing and transmuting energy from a place.

Angels: I call in angelic forces not so much for clearing energy, but rather for healing and light work in the space or home when all the residual energy has left. Clearing energy in an area can leave holes or weak spots in an area once residual energy is gone, so calling in angels for healing will help restore the energy or aura of the space with light energy, which will be beneficial. Calling in angels that specialize in transmuting energy or healing energy works most effectively in my experience. I usually call in forces that work with Archangel Raphael and Archangel Uriel, but call in those that you find work best with you.

Elementals: Elementals oversee activity and energy of the Earth, so it's best to ask for permission from elemental energy to stimulate the energy of the Earth's aura before and during your work. Elementals aren't going to care much about the universal energies or spirit energies that you work with; rather they will oversee the clearing of environmental objects and lower vibrational energy associated with the Earth's auric field. Elemental entities will usually come in to oversee your energy work. Their main purpose is to make sure we don't make mistakes and damage environmental energy. Healing elementals might also visit depending on how damaging the residual energy was. While angelic healers work on the higher vibrational energy connected with spiritual fields, healing elemental entities will come to heal lower levels associated with Earth energy. These healing elemental energies usually do not show themselves to you visually but rather may present themselves through Earth, air, fire, or water manifestations. Examples include a strong burning flame or heavy smoke when you smudge, a sunny day turns into a rainy day quickly, wind may blow heavily to clear away energy or trees, and plants may help stimulate the energy in a space. While I do my clearing work, I call in elemental entities by asking for energies of the Earth, Air, Fire, and Water to come in and oversee clearing work and to receive their blessings.

Protectors: After all the portal doors in the building or space are closed, residual energy is cleared, and the energetic holes or weaknesses are healed, I call in angelic protectors to stand guard over the space. This is to ensure negative spiritual energy or heavy residual energy cannot return to the space once we have left. You may feel the presence of a strong and powerful guard that stands over the property, or you may feel a very high and loving presence to comfort and shield the space. Just know the angelic energy that comes through knows what's best for that environment. Don't be surprised if they stand guard with elemental entities. Depending on the type of situation that brought in the original negative forces, you may need extra assistance to shield against more negative energy coming in. I normally use two forms of physical protection to help the angelic and elemental guards. These two forms of protection are salt barriers or circles and protective crystal grids.

Borders and Shields

Salt Circles: In order to form a border or shield against negative energy, mediums or clearers will sometimes create a circle around the property with salt. As stated before, salt is great for neutralizing energy, but it also carries a high absorbing force that allows you to set thought and intent in the salt. While sprinkling the salt in a circle formation around a property, set protective intent into the salt. Affirmations or prayers for protection work well, or just thinking about shielding negative spirits away can be effective. As I mentioned previously, remember that salt is corrosive, so be careful where you spread the salt so that it doesn't damage structures around the property.

Crystal grids: By itself or in conjunction with salt barriers, a crystal energy grid is great in helping promote a healing and protective environment after you clear residual energy. A crystal grid is an arrangement of crystals on a specific geometric shape that focuses on stimulating energy for a particular purpose. Arrange the crystal grid in the geometric shape that works best for the protective intent. I highly recommend researching and experimenting to find the most efficient protective patterns. The center of the grid can be placed in the area of the most activity in the home and stretch out the grid far past the parameters of the space so that the whole area is protected. Just be aware of your surroundings and not accidentally go into someone else's property. Grids are also a great way to close and lock spiritual doors. Use smaller protective grids over a space that had a strong spiritual door for extra protection. Doors are less likely to reopen or reappear if spirits can't manipulate the energy in the space due to the strength of the crystal grid. Each grid has specific crystals assigned to them, so be sure to investigate the type of energy stimulation you want before purchasing the grid. The grid will tell you the type of crystals to use. If you plan on creating your own grid, do research on high vibrational and energy clearing crystals to see which crystals work best for you.

Now that we've assessed the situation, closed all portal doors, cleared all residual energy, left protective barriers, and asked for spiritual assistance, we can now leave the space knowing that we've done all we can for the day. Be aware that even with powerful tools, abilities, and assistance, it may take a few days for all of the remaining energy to dissipate. I always tell my clients to leave out salt, crystals, and play high vibrational music for at least three days after the clearing to reinforce the work I've already done. If the occupants are still having issues after the three-day period, you can come back to do more energy clearing work. Every time you return to the location, the energy should feel lighter and clearer. If it doesn't, I would double check areas that might have been missed for hidden doors or vortexes.

CHAPTER ELEVEN

Types of Earthbound Spirits

There are many different types of earthbound spirits that you will be working with and connecting to. Because of this, you need to be educated on the various levels of energy involved in our work and the types of spirits that reside within these levels. To begin with, not all earthbound spirits reside at the same vibration. Spirits reside in a vibrational level that correlates to the emotional and mental state of the spirit. This means that spirits with heavier mental and emotional baggage reside at a lower, denser vibration than spirits with less density, yet they will still all be earthbound and reside within the in-between levels of existence.

Within the levels of existence are the in-between states. These in-between states have many levels of vibration within themselves. The vibrational levels change as you ascend to higher levels. So, the lower the level, the slower and denser it is, the higher the level, the faster and lighter it is. Each level the spirit resides in changes or ascends slightly to a faster and lighter vibration as emotional, mental, and psychological issues are removed or resolved. This is why emotional and mental counseling of the spirit is essential to their transition. By helping spirits alleviate issues, their vibration becomes lighter, making it easier to ascend to a higher level of existence or what we call "crossing over."

Elements of the Soul

In addition to the variances of vibrational levels of earthbound spirits, there are also elements of the soul that may get fractured. This may dictate why the spirit is earthbound and how it detached from its predestined plan of crossing over. The soul is fluid, expansive, and immeasurable. It is a conjunction of various levels of perception and experiences. The soul itself is mainly combined of five elements. The mental, the emotional, the physiological, the karmic, and the higher self. All of these elements are parts of the soul that can form together or expand and depart from the source.

The Mental

The mental state of the soul is connected to all consciousness related to the mind. All the memories of people, places, and events get stored in the mind through various parts of the consciousness. The mind can be fractured on many different levels depending on the state of awareness and perception. Do not confuse the mind with the physical brain. The brain is an organ within the body that regulates functions and controls the systems of the body. The mind itself is a complex form of structured consciousness and sub-consciousness that is housed in the brain to relay information to the body and soul. All thoughts from the human experience are stored in the mind of the soul, which transfers to the higher consciousness or collective consciousness on the "otherside." All of these thoughts of the mind are being transferred to the collective consciousness all the time, even while alive. In death, the mind of the soul gets to merge back in with your higher consciousness to download all information that's been collected. If the mental element of the soul is fractured by anguish, pain, or suffering that is too much for the mind to handle, it can separate from the rest of the soul and become earthbound. Much like a shattered crystal, the shards remain. Part of the mind can also create separate entity forms that originate from those thought patterns. Split personalities, negative manifestations, or projections of mental disorders can tear the mental soul apart, leaving various imprints of the mind in the Earth plane.

The Emotional

The emotional form of the soul can be easily confused with the mental. Every time you have an emotional experience, you use your mind to express through the emotion. But the emotion itself comes from the part of the soul that feels, not thinks. Feelings from your life and other lives get stored in the emotional element of the soul. Don't you ever wonder where phobias come from? They are stored emotional responses within the soul to stimulation from an event whether in this life or in another. This response to the event gets stored in the emotional level of the soul. If a particular event in death is too emotional for the soul to experience, an emotional fracture can take place, separating from the other collective parts of the soul. This fractured emotional element can wander the Earth plane, separated from the rest of the soul on the other side until the emotions are healed enough to merge back with the higher self.

The Physiological

The physiological part of the soul connects the soul through biology dealing with the functions and activities of the human body and their parts, including all physical and chemical processes. This would be the "prana" or "breathe of spirit" that is housed within the body, connecting all biological and chemical actions within. It's the way for the soul to connect in with the physical body. The aura or energy field of the body is generated through the physiological connection of the soul to the body. People who have died very quickly can disconnect with the body, leaving behind the physiological shell until the body has completely shut down. Many people have seen the soul leave the body before death. Fractions or elements of the soul leave early so that other elements are not influenced by the pain of death. The physiological part of the soul stays behind until complete death has occurred. Once death is complete, the physiological element merges back in the higher self. The physiological element of the soul is rarely earthbound on its own without another fragmented form of the soul. You may see the apparition of a person around the scene of a tragic accident before it ascends to a higher state of being. The apparition is the soul's connection to the body, leaving an imprint of the body's form within its energy. In some instances, apparitions of ghosts that are seen in the paranormal community are the physiological part of the soul with other remaining fragments such as the mental and emotional aspects of the person.

The Karmic

The karmic element of the soul is the cause and effect where intent and actions of an individual are determined. The karmic effect of past lives can influence the structure of a person's life purpose, leaving the soul to search out situations to balance out this karma. This part of the soul determines many details of a person's life such as people they meet, situations they face, or places they travel to. Everything from a person's life will play a part in balancing out karma from an individual's energy. The karmic element can fracture at death depending on how strong the karmic effect has on the individual. If someone were an abuser in another life, they may wish to be born into an abusive family, understanding how they affected other people through the experience of the pain themselves. If the karmic element of the soul determines that they aren't ready to experience the pain and suffering themselves and decides to run from the experience, the soul may stay behind at death, unforgiving of themselves for not learning the lesson.

The Higher Self

The Higher Self, or what people like to call your divine self, resides on the other side while you are alive. This is the form of the soul that oversees all activity within your life and connects it back to the higher consciousness. Some people also refer to this as the spirit of the soul. Whichever term you like to use, just know it's the higher part of the soul that connects in with the higher forms of consciousness. The higher self then sends the information back down to the rest of the soul through the consciousness or subconscious. All parts of the soul are then influenced by this information. When a person dies, all elements of the soul merge back in with the higher self to complete the union of the soul back to spirit. The higher self will never be earthbound because it never leaves the higher states of consciousness. When an element of the soul is earthbound, the higher self tries to connect in with other parts of the soul, though most efforts are lost due to the mental, emotional, or karmic trauma of the soul. Perceptions are clouded by negative illusions, weakening the connection to the higher self. It's the role of a rescue medium to connect all elements of the soul back together and merge it back with the higher self for healing.

Categories of Earthbound Spirits

I would like to explain the types of earthbound spirits that reside in certain levels as categories. This helps create a better understanding of the different spirits you will work with. Try to remember that even though I group these spirits together into categories, they each have their own personal vibration and reasoning for being earthbound.

Category 1

The first category of earthbound spirits carries a lighter and faster vibration that resides just under the astral plane of existence. These earthbound spirits will reside at higher levels because they carry less spiritual baggage. These spirits are often less of a threat and more in need of counseling and encouragement from clearers or mediums. For those who are new to rescue work, it's best to ask your spiritual team to help maintain a level of security that only allows category 1 spirits into your vibration until you learn more protection techniques or become more comfortable around more negative spirits. Category 1 spirits that reside in the higher in-between states would normally consist of:

Lost: People who have died and for some reason could not find their way to the other side. Their death may have been sudden, or they may have been afraid of the transition at the time and turned away from it. The clouded perception of a negative experience from death could have hindered their transition, leaving them without a clear path to take. The white light or door to the other side is hidden from them because their vibration is too low to notice it. Examples of situations that may create a lost soul are: car crash, drowning, accidental overdose, or sickness. The elements of the soul that may be lost are mental and/or emotional. The karmic element is less likely to be influenced by this situation and will most likely merge in with the higher self at death. You won't have to do a lot of counseling during these types of rescues because they just need a guide to point them in the right direction. Bringing in guides from the other side are useful at this time to put the soul's mind at ease.

Confused: You may come across souls that are confused with the death process. Certain cultures or religions teach us how death works, such as who will come to get us and how we ascend to heaven or manifest in spirit. When things do not align due to the teachings of these influences, the soul may get confused and turn their back during the transition. This situation occurs less and less as we expand our awareness into the individual experience of death and see it less to be a "one size fits all" scenario.

Other confused souls may have had a tragic death that happened so suddenly, they did not realize that they died. I've had a great many people perplexed by this. How can someone not know they are dead? Well, how do you know you are asleep when you are? Doesn't everything seem real to you when you dream? Are you aware of the conscious condition and that you are not awake during this period? The answer is, probably not. Our mind is wired to perceive and respond to stimulation around us, regardless of its reality. If a person dies in a sudden situation, the mind can get lost in the tragic event, which plays over and over again until there is a break in the awareness of the mind. It's sort of like waking someone out of a dream. Until you break the continual cycle of mental thought, the soul will wander around in the moment, unaware of their own death. In some instances, this loop can play for years, even centuries in rare cases.

Lonely or Sad: As hard as it is to imagine, there are many lonely people in the world. This may include the homeless, the abused, or the lost—those who perceive themselves to be forgotten. They suffer from the disconnection to people around them. We all need someone, even though we go through moments of wanting to be alone. The soul comes from a collective consciousness that is connected to everyone else. We all feel the need to be connected and loved. When we live a life of loneliness it can affect us in such a way that restricts the soul from connecting back to the greater consciousness. This can lead to disconnection on many levels. Emotions can hinder our natural ability to transition back to a loving embrace. Pain and heartache from a life of separation may cause the soul to weaken and fracture. The spirit hindered by this emotional element may become earthbound until counseling is completed.

Stubborn: We all know that one stubborn person who just won't let go of something or someone. They are set in their ways and have no need to change to appease anyone or anything else around them. The same situation can occur after death. There will be souls that refuse to let go of their life because of various reasons. They might have worked really hard to accomplish something, and they aren't ready to let go yet. Or, they might have such a deep connection with someone they aren't ready to leave yet. There are many different scenarios that can influence a spirit to turn away from their transition. It's pure stubbornness that keeps them earthbound. The dying process doesn't change the person's ego or personality immediately, as this is done after crossing over through past-life review, counseling, and healing with your guides and angels.

Indifferent: Life can be rather harsh for some, leaving people numb or empty inside. Their feelings for others or cares regarding events in the world are forgotten due to emotional pain or mental conditioning. People can be so fed up with life that they become indifferent. They have no feelings or emotions left for people or situations. This is no different in death. The thought of crossing into the light holds no meaning for them. They turn their back on the positive stimulus and focus on nothing but emptiness. This is where many mediums call the "gray zone." It's where spirits have lost their way and have no desire to find their way into the light. The emotional element of the soul disconnects from the mental element, leaving the soul impartial to situations that are in their best interest. The rescuer's job is to connect these elements back together and heal the wounds of the lost wanderer.

Scared: We can only imagine what the mind must endure during a traumatic situation for a child, young adult, or victim of abuse, neglect, or force. The situations they face can deeply affect the mind, the emotions, and the soul's karmic connection all at once. Because of this, the soul may fracture into many parts, leaving the soul disconnected and scared. The soul may stay together at times to play the event over and over again, but then fractures at times when it becomes too intense. What might seem during a haunting to be more than one spirit, is actually the same spirit projecting out different elements in different locations. This is when the rescue medium might have to counsel each element separately so that it can connect back to the higher self for structured healing from guides and angels.

Category 2

Category 2 would consist of spirits that carry more emotional baggage such as anger, frustration, jealousy, or resentment. Negative behavior and emotional attachments can create a sense of fear and anxiety, which carry a heavier vibration than those in category 1. The vast majority of these spirits aren't evil or hurtful; rather they are more emotionally and mentally compromised, which may lead some to lash out in anger or fear. Category 2 spirits are highly likely to attach to the living for various reasons. In most cases, these spirits are aware of their death, but despite the loving sensation of the white light, turn from it. What follows is a list of category 2 spirits that you may come in contact with.

Angry or Hurt: Anger can be extremely hard to control for some individuals. Situations in your life that cause painful or hurtful feelings often lead to anger. These spirits could have experienced various stressful situations such as a break-up, move, loss of a loved one, difficult relationships, arguments, loss of a job or financial security, and so on. Anger over the painful situation can make the spirit resentful against everything, including the white light. Anger can make even the best of us do things we would highly regret afterward because of uncontrolled emotions. Spirits filled with anger, hurt, or resentment commonly reflect that energy onto people in the physical world, which is why they feel negative. We must remember that this is only a temporary emotion and that the person is not a negative person. By connecting and communicating with these spirits, we can understand the reason for the anger and try to eliminate it through counseling and healing techniques. There can be times when spirits just need to talk to someone and get things "off their chest" in order to move on. Closure becomes very important in the transition for these spirits. By clearing away the anger or hurt, the spirit can lift their vibration, connecting them back into the white light.

Jealous: Jealousy can lead to many destructive behaviors and may cause spirits to turn away from the white light until they can let go of feelings of entitlement or bitterness. The human psyche or mind creates a form of self through the ego. The ego determines who you are and how you see yourself in the world. Spirits that have a strong and powerful ego will hold onto feelings of resentment or jealousy after death because they believed they should have had something or someone in their life. You really need to understand where jealousy originates from to help the spirit detach from the mental and emotional entrapment. Did the person believe that they deserved more in their life? Did they regret that someone close to them received more love and attention than they did? Did a competitive relationship that ended in loss create a feeling of failure? Determining this will help give you ideas for effective counseling. Even though you may feel that the jealousy is unjustified because of egotistical behavior from the spirit, you must understand that this spirit is trying to learn from the experience. New souls do not understand that by letting go of all wants and needs, you become free from the negative ego. They must learn this over time. So saying "just get over it" isn't always going to help.

Vain: Being vain is having or showing an excessively high opinion of one's appearance, abilities, or worth. This can make a person come across as negative or full of themselves. By understanding why people seem or act vain will help with this situation. Vanity usually comes from a place of self-doubt, insecurities, and feelings of failure. I know that sounds like the opposite of what the person is displaying, but most egotistical behavior, such as vanity, is an excessive form of overcompensation. If someone thinks very little of themselves or feels insecure, they may act out or "show off" to make themselves appear more appealing to others. Talking highly of themselves is a defense mechanism to protect against any attacks on them. If they convince themselves that they are above all others, then no one can harm them. This is common behavior of someone who lacks self-worth. You need to understand that what someone projects isn't always the truth; rather it is a projection of an emotion, good or bad. Learning how to empathize with those with low self-esteem will help in your rescue work.

Manipulative: Manipulation is a commonly formed behavior that provokes another person to do something against their will, usually derived from resentment, entitlement, jealousy, anger, or frustration. Manipulative spirits believe that they can control everyone or everything around them. Manipulative spirits with negative emotions are some of the most common forms of spirit attachments. They try to get people here in the physical world to do whatever they want, even if it ends up harming the physical "host." Spirits with natural or learned behaviors that harm others should be handled with strong reinforcements from your spiritual team as you are more likely to clear them from people rather than helping them into the light. It isn't until several layers of negative emotions are cleared that this type of spirit will become open to counsel or help. Angelic healers are your strongest allies at this time.

Mental Disorders: Spirits that handled life through challenging mental disorders will likely take this challenge with them into the spirit world. Since it's common for spirits to mold their astral bodies based on the belief of who they were mentally and emotionally, the form of the destructive disorder can and will determine who and what they are in the spirit world. All realities pertaining to the spirit usually have some fraction of pain and suffering of the mental disorder. Those with bipolar disorder or severe anxiety disorder may continue to suffer through these emotional torments and will seem rather negative in nature, though most are not harmful to those in the physical world. People with strong split-personality disorders may show several fractured personalities in spirit as if they are several spirits. It's very common for people with these disorders to become earthbound as they do not think or feel clearly enough to comprehend the change from a physical body to the astral body. People who are already lost in the abyss of their mind may never truly understand the difference and may wander for years before they are rescued. These types of spirits must be handled with great sensitivity. I recommend only connecting to the spirit long enough to bridge the gap between spirit and spirit healers/guides on the other side. Allow advanced healers in the spiritual world to handle these kinds of spirits by helping the spirit cross into the white light. It can sometimes be more harmful to get involved with these spirits as they need someone with proper training in their disorder to help. Becoming the mediator between spirit and guide is sometimes enough to help them find their way.

Drug Abuse: Spirits that are earthbound that may have passed from a drug addiction overdose are most likely looking for resolution or forgiveness. The act of taking their own life through the means of a substance may be too much for a person to comprehend. A great deal of people who died from drug addiction did so accidentally, never expecting that they would pass into the spirit world. Spirits wandering the Earth plane following a death from drug addiction most likely need to find peace within themselves to move on. Rescue mediums serve as healers by listening and empathizing with them. Also, spirits may move into the light once a message is relayed to their family, usually in a form of an apology. Of course there are a few spirits that move into spirit with severe addictions that never seem to end. These spirits search out those here in the physical world with the same addiction as their own to attach to. By attaching onto a person in physical form, they can experience the effects of the drug through their host. In many cases, these spirits influence people to crave drugs or substances that are more harmful, leaving the host susceptible to death as well. Once their host moves into spirit through death, the influencing spirit moves on to another living host to complete the cycle again, doing this over and over again as the addiction grows. These types of spirits need more clearing work with healers and spirit police on the other side. They need to be reconstructed and healed of their addiction, which can only be done through advanced spiritual healers. Try to keep your distance from these spirits while doing the clearing work.

Abused or Tortured: There are no words to describe the pain and suffering that victims can experience through severe abuse and torture. The immense emotional, mental, and physical harm that these people experience can never be understood until you've lived through severe abuse yourself. These types of spirits must be handled carefully so that you will not harm the spirit further. The pain of the abuse can easily alter the perception of the spirit, creating an altered reality shaped from the fear of the abuse. Spirits can get trapped in a state of suffering, never escaping their endless ordeal of sadness and fear. All counseling and healing work must be done slowly and delicately so that the spirit can adapt to the new vibration within their own comfort level. Do not be surprised if these spirits try to attack you in response to your rescue. It's very common for those who have been hurt to defend themselves if they should feel threatened. This is not to harm you, rather to protect themselves.

Murdered: Spirits that endured the painful experience of murder will most likely hold a very low vibrational frequency. The act of murder itself carries a low vibration. The combination of the act plus the emotional pain and suffering creates a very negative environment around the spirit. I don't want there to be confusion surrounding all murders. Not all murder victims become earthbound. Angelic healers and guides stand closely by the spirits to help them transition, especially during tragic events. It isn't until the spirit becomes overwhelmed by sadness, anger, and pain that they turn from the white light. You need to understand that not all people face the same situation the same way mentally and emotionally. Spirits with a strong and positive sense of self will be just fine and will find the white light easily. Other spirits that are weaker mentally and emotionally can become more compromised and afraid. They turn from the white light and become surrounded by an environment created from pain and suffering. All light and guidance is no longer visible to the spirit and they become lost in the moment of their death. It's the job of the rescue medium to help surround this spirit with healing and comforting energy. Changing the environment around the spirit slowly will help them to perceive a different reality which will help them to find their way into the light.

Category 3

Category 3 would consist of negative-minded individuals who harassed and harmed people here in the physical world, continuing their spree of abuse in the spirit world. Common types of spirits would be rapists, abusers, criminals, murderers, or anyone with negative or harassing tendencies. A great many of these spirits weren't born negative. Life just had a way of influencing them in such a way that made them make bad decisions. Spirits may have been abused themselves, or they may have had their heart broken. Negative events can change a person, recreating them into the mirror image of the pain that hurt them in the first place. There are others who were born with natural addictions to negative behavior. These types of spirits would be less open to counseling and support; rather they would need more forceful clearing and healing work to be done. Working heavily with protectors and healers in the spirit world is essential while connecting to these earthbound spirits.

Abusers: Abusers can either be born or created. People born with abusive tendencies have a greater chance of afflicting damage onto others. They were born with the urge to control and harm others around them. Usually, these abusers are mentally unstable. They abuse and torture people around them, usually through acts of sexual, physical, or mental harm feeding into a psychological addiction that the abuser cannot control. Abusers who are created by suffering through abuse themselves have mental and emotional scars that can influence them to do harm upon others due to pain and anger. By allowing someone else to suffer the pain they endured, they can release their frustrations. Regardless of why a person abuses someone else, the end result always ends up with someone suffering. Quite often these abusers have disconnected themselves from the deeper connection to other people. They have no moral judgement or empathy for others. People become more like objects to them that they can control and manipulate. Those who take the anger and frustration with them into the spirit world will find themselves continuing the abuse upon those either in spirit or the physical world. Yes, spirits can and do abuse other spirits. There have been cases of abusers that kill their victims through a murder suicide, that will then hold their victim hostage and continue the abuse in the spirit world. This is when rescuers and clearing specialists need to request the help of very powerful healers and protectors in the spirit world for assistance not only to handle the abusers, but also help the victims under the control of the abuser.

Sexual Addictions: Sexual addictions can be seen in the same way as a drug addiction or mental disorder since there are many forms of sexual addiction. People with addictive tendencies may also become addicted to sexual experiences because, just like drug addiction, it stimulates a natural high of endorphins that the body craves. People sense a need or urgency to repeatedly perform these sexual acts to experience this "high" over and over again. Those affected with sexual mental disorders find themselves desiring sexual activity much more than most people. They have a hard time controlling their urge to perform sexual acts and may search out victims to appease their desires. Individuals who move into the spirit world with strong sexual desires usually hold a much lower vibration because they are focusing on a very physical act. Physical energy is much lower than spiritual energy. By concentrating on a physical act repeatedly, they lower their vibration and search out people in the physical world to have sexual encounters with. Spirits with sexual addictions are very likely to attach to victims with low self-esteem, those who are sick or immobile, or people with other addictive behaviors. Rescue mediums act more as clearers for these spirits since most are not ready for their transition until they overcome their physical addiction. Working heavily with spiritual healers and protectors is extremely encouraged.

Murderers: Just like any other scenario, murderers do not all have the same motive for their act. Murder can occur through acts of rage, aggression, or sadness; or they can be completely accidental. Judging someone on the fact that they murdered someone solely on the fact that they are evil is not appropriate. Quite often these spirits that hold back from the white light after a murder find themselves judging their own act with shame and dishonor. The guilt is what binds them to Earth. The white light has a way of merging in with the spirit at the time of death, which can make the spirit understand the error of their act. By connecting in with Divine energy that surrounds them with unconditional love, they understand what they did was wrong and painful. If the spirit decides at that moment to turn away from the white light because they do not feel worthy, they become earthbound until they can face and forgive themselves.

Sadists: There are people who for some reason only wish to inflict pain upon others. People who become serial killers find murdering others to be a form of addictive behavior that allows the murderer to experience pleasure in the act. These types of people most often have a mental disorder that controls their vindictive behavior. They cannot be controlled or counseled from their behavior as this is something that is embedded into their consciousness and ego. Spirits with these behaviors that have murdered many people might hide from the white light, not from shame, but from judgement they will not face. They do not believe they have done wrong, therefore, turn away from Divine energy like an angered child from a loving parent. Disconnection from the Divine will motivate the spirit to move into lower dimensional energy. Rescue mediums will only act as clearers for these spirits. Spirits may disguise themselves to you in demonic ways to make themselves look more powerful and gain control over others. Working heavily with spirit police and healers is mandatory. Shielding and protection techniques should be used at all times.

Satanists or Devil Worshippers: Individuals who perform acts of Satanic rituals or devil worship lower their energy vibration when connecting in with demonic entities. Usually these people start performing rituals out of curiosity and become overcome by demonic entities that compel them to continue these rituals over and over. Opening spiritual doors and vortexes through these rituals will also create negative energy in their space. Those looking to perform rituals to control others or to manifest negative entities for their own pleasure will often fall victim to these entities themselves. Quite often these demonic entities will make the person performing the ritual commit suicide so that they can continue to control the person in death. The energy of this person that moves into spirit is so low, the energy of the white light is hidden because the vibration is too high to perceive. The entities will also shield or deceive the spirit from the white light, trapping them in a dark and negative plane of consciousness. These spirits are usually influenced by dark energy, forcing them to harass and harm people in spirit and the physical world. However, just like any spirit they have the power of free will. If for any reason they decide that they do not want to be in a negative environment and turn to the energy of the Divine, their energy vibration naturally raises up and connects them to angelic help, allowing them to be healed. Rescuers who work with spirits with demonic entities attached to them or carry a very low demonic energy vibration should seek out a demonologist or someone experienced with very low vibrational entities. As a general rule, you should never work in this field of rescue work without a very powerful protector in the spirit world.

CHAPTER TWELVE
Direct Rescue

Developing and working as a rescue medium will come naturally to those who were born to do this type of work, and connecting to earthbound spirits will occur regularly. Mediums with a strong energy pull to earthbound spirits won't have trouble connecting and might have spirits around them all the time. It's what I like to call "the beacon" effect. Myself and others like me send out an energy pulse that is very different from other mediums. This beacon or energy vibration connects at the same vibrational level as an earthbound spirit. Once the connection is made, spirits are drawn to us like a magnet. I have heard other mediums liken it to the analogy of a bug to a light. People with our abilities are the light, and the earthbound spirits are the bugs. This analogy may sound harsh, but it's quite literally the same situation.

Keep in mind that not all spirits will be drawn to mediums. The effect all depends on distance to the medium and the environment the spirit resides in. Rescue work is mainly done through two styles: direct and indirect. The difference is in the link to spirit and the close proximity to where the spirit is located. Most direct rescues will occur when the spirit is close by, and the medium can make a strong direct link to them. Once the connection is made, the communication, counseling, and guidance can begin. I'd like to think that direct rescue work is done in three different ways.

1. The spirit finds you.
2. You get called into an active area with an earthbound spirit.
3. Someone with a spirit attachment finds you for help.

Direct rescue is just like it sounds. You directly connect in with the spirit to help aid in their transition or clear them from people or places (if needed). Both of these situations get handled differently depending on the spirit and the reason for their earthbound status. Let's first examine what can happen when the spirit finds you first and what to do once the connection is made.

The Earthbound Spirit Finds You

Quite often earthbound spirits will connect with a medium close by to their place of death or the place they believe will offer resolution. If you happen to walk by a restaurant where a person was killed and the earthbound spirit is searching for resolution, it's very possible that this earthbound spirit will connect to you because it notices your energy. Why? It's because mediums carry a slightly higher vibration than most people. The medium's vibration is very close to the proximity of the earthbound spirit's vibration. Because of this, the earthbound spirit "sees" the medium better than most other people. Once the earthbound spirit merges with your vibration, they can often find out things about you such as your abilities and skills. They will find a way to communicate with you through your energy.

Other situations similar to the bug and light analogy can occur. If a wandering spirit comes across your "light" vibration, it will be drawn to you and try to connect in with you. It's true that some spirits may take their time communicating. These are the spirits that just like to sit back and watch. They are looking for a familiar or comfortable energy to draw close in with so that they do not feel alone. Don't be surprised if you find yourself surrounded by countless earthbound spirits for this reason. Loneliness can compel spirits to follow you regardless of other factors, simply because they want to be near you. It's difficult for me to describe the number of experiences I've had with spirits simply looking for companionship.

So now that you know why spirits may come to you, it's best to know when spirits will most likely try connect in with you. Not everyone will have the same experience, though I find that most mediums connect in with earthbound spirits during these "peak times."

When You Are Sleeping

Oh boy, get ready for sleepless nights! I can't even begin to explain how many nights I was up all night talking to spirits or fighting off spirit attacks. Sleeping is the most common time of day when spirits connect. It really makes perfect sense. The part of the mind that handles dreaming also controls active visualization, daydreams, meditations, astral travel, and imagination. The mind is an active playground for spirits through mental mediumship. Not only do dreams open up our mind for visualization, it also brings us down into the subconscious level where spirits can connect to us. In general, it can be harder for spirits to connect to us through our daily activities such as work, chores, paying bills, taking care of kids, etc. Our mind is simply too busy thinking! It's the time when our mind stops thinking that the spirits have wiggle room for communication. This is why meditation is so useful to mediumship. The logical thinking required by daily activities overpowers the right-sided imagination and visualization. Sleeping not only allows spirit to connect with our minds, but it also lowers the vibration of our energy to a stable and comfortable level where spirits do not feel overwhelmed. Remaining busy all day can overstimulate the spirit, so they usually wait until our energy is more quiet.

Daydreaming

Yes, we are all guilty of doing it from time to time. Those who daydream more often have a greater chance of spirit communication. The windows of your mind open to allow a flow of spirit energy when you daydream. Most mediums with clairvoyance ability can connect in with spirits through daydreaming or meditation. It's our visual communication with spirits. The hardest part of mediumship is telling the difference between your daydream and spirit communication. How can we tell if it's real? Well, that usually is accomplished through experience, feeling the spirit at the same time, getting validation for the messages, or just plain trust. Even the best mediums in the field need validation of the spirit because it's sometimes hard to tell the difference between spirit connection or your mind creating an image. The best way I can tell the difference between the two is when the spirit addresses me directly. The spirit will literally look at me, talk to me, and I'll feel the energy connection between us. Everyone will have their own way of telling the difference. If you are ever in doubt, start talking to the spirit and ask for more information. This is a two-way conversation. They like to be talked to just as much as they like talking to you. So, chat away.

Time Alone

Spirits most often will wait until you are alone to make contact. The heavy energy from the surrounding people may overwhelm the spirit, or they may not feel comfortable around them. Your pulse or beacon of energy sends out a message that they can trust you. The average person does not have this vibration, so don't be surprised if spirits won't connect in with you while others are around. Instances of these occurrences include when you are driving, getting dressed, or as creepy as it sounds, showering. Yes, I have had that experience!

When You're Open During an Intuitive or Mediumship Class

Well, this makes perfect sense. You're open and ready to communicate, so why wouldn't an earthbound spirit make contact? Just remember that making a connection to spirits on the other side needs a higher vibration, so earthbound spirits won't connect to you when you're on "higher ground." When your vibration starts to lower a bit when you ground, earthbound spirits may slip in and quickly connect in before you shut down.

Gatekeeper

Not all spirit communication is going to happen when you want it to. Quite often, spirits get pushy and demand your attention even when you are busy in the physical world. Much like children craving for your attention, spirits will shout out to you even when you're on a date or demand your attention when you are entertaining guests. Anything can be interrupted if you let the spirit communication get out of control. This is when you need to set up your boundaries. You are in full control of every spirit connection. By setting up your boundaries, you let your gatekeeper know when and where you are free to communicate with earthbound spirits. Your gatekeeper is your spiritual guide that allows the spirits to come and connect with you. Think of it like a bouncer at a night club that regulates who can come in and dance. The gatekeeper decides who gets to connect and who doesn't. They work with you to protect you and make sure your needs get met as well. Remember, the gatekeeper can't do anything without your request, as it would go against your free will.

Setting up a meeting with your gatekeeper is useful in creating boundary requests. This is usually done through meditation or requests made from affirmations. Boundary requests to the gatekeeper should accumulate in a way so that you do not become overwhelmed with spirit activity, but still allow time for spirits to get the help they need. Suggestions for boundaries would include the following.

Time to Connect

When are you free to connect to earthbound spirits? Early in the morning or late at night? Are you okay to connect when you are driving or cooking? Think about when you are the most able to help a spirit without having many distractions around you.

Places to Connect

Are there certain rooms in your home that you do not want spirits to enter? Do you want to protect small children or keep spirits out of the bathroom for privacy? These would be things to consider. Do you even want earthbound spirits in your home? Homes are considered sacred spaces that allow you to feel safe. Do you feel comfortable enough having unknown earthbound spirits follow you home? Maybe setting up special spirit zones will help, like a small park in your area or the beach. It should always be a place where you feel safe and protected.

People Around You When You Connect

Do you want earthbound spirits connecting with you when you are with family and friends, or do you want to be alone? Do you mind spirits connecting with you when you are surrounded by people at church or a metaphysical center? Spirits will sometimes insist on communication, and we don't want to seem rude and turn away from them, but they need to get the point that not everyone is going to understand what you do. It's best to protect yourself when you are around people who might judge you.

How You Feel When You Connect

It's good practice to connect with spirits when you are feeling your best. Feeling sick, drained, upset, or overwhelmed may make it difficult to do your work, and it certainly isn't the best time for you. Taking time for yourself to heal is important. Letting your gatekeeper know how you feel will help. Feeling sick or upset only gets worse when you have to take on the trauma, depression, sadness, or anger from earthbound spirits. Allow yourself to rest.

Communication

Once we've set up our boundaries, we're now able to have a safe, secure, and stress-free environment for spirit communication, which happens to be the first part of spirit rescue. Communication with earthbound spirits is the most essential aspect of rescue work. How else would we know what to do? Just pointing them into the light isn't always the best strategy. Would that work if the spirit isn't aware of their death and has no idea what the white light is? Probably not. So getting a good sense of who the spirit is, what they need for resolution, and how they can transition is extremely important. The most common information acquired in communication from an earthbound spirit is:

- Who the spirit is.
- How the spirit died.
- Personality of the spirit.
- What background or culture do they come from?
- What is the spirit's intent?
- Is it a fractured part of the soul?
- Emotional and mental state of the spirit.
- Most immediate influence around the spirit.

- Are they alone or with other spirits?
- What are they looking for or need?
- Are they aware of their current situation?
- Are there any entities or other spirits influencing their decision making?

You may need to document some of this information to help you with your decision making. If the spirit decides to leave and come back another time, you'll have it all written down, and you'll be ready to receive more information. Not all spirits will be open to communications with you. It may take time for earthbound spirits to trust you or feel open enough to share intimate details with you. So, a part of this acquired information happens when you merge with the spirit and have an energy transfer. But do be aware that you'll sometimes need to go through the spirit's energetic layers in order to obtain this information.

Energetic Layers

Just like the living have an auric field of layers, spirits have layers of energy. Within each layer of energy houses imprints of the situations that the spirit may be facing as well as aspects of the soul. The most recent events would be projected out onto the top layers, such as their illness or death. Getting through the layers of energy can be difficult depending on how strong the emotional or mental attachments are to the layers. The amount of layering the spirit expresses depends on who the spirit is, what they've been through, and what they are aware of. The more trauma and emotional baggage the spirit carries, the more layers you'll have to get through. The most common layers a spirit carries are:

Outer Layer

Emotions, typically negative in nature: This layer can consist of fear, anxiety, aggression, anger, lust, hate, vengeance, sadness, and loss. These emotions would be layered on the spirit like a heavy blanket. Penetrating these emotions can be difficult because you're probably going to experience them yourself if you are an empath or clairsentient. Knowing when to step out of the emotional layer when you become overwhelmed is important. Remember to have control over the situation. We don't want to become emotionally compromised ourselves.

Second Layer

Mental thoughts would be housed in this layer: What the spirit thinks about themselves, others, and their situation would be expressed. This is when you get a sense of what the spirit knows. Typically, spirits will try to block you from reading certain aspects about their life depending on whether they feel you will judge them or not. Letting them know that you aren't there to judge; rather helping them on their personal spiritual journey instead is needed.

Third Layer

Desires or intent will be focused. Once you can break through the emotional and mental layers, the spirit's true colors will show through. What does the spirit want or desire? Do they want to make amends? Do they need to tell someone goodbye? Are they still holding onto a lost relationship? This information will help you determine what counseling and guidance will be needed for the spirit to let go and make their transition.

Fourth Layer

The spirit's current life's impact on the spirit will be examined. What kind of life did they have? How did they view themselves in the world? Do they feel they had a successful life? Until they do a full-life review, the information stored here will be the most current expression the spirit has looking back on their life. It's vitally important for the spirit to start making amends and let go of any regret attained during their life. This closure will help the spirit release into the transition process to complete their full-life review and healing on the other side.

Innermost Layer

The innermost layer is the soul's connection to the higher self and all karmic connections to other lives. This core layer connects the spirit to all lives that they have experienced and impacts the decision making of the soul in the current lifetime. The current ego and personality of the individual in the current life isn't noticed as much because you connect in with the higher divine self of the spirit. Many mediums may call this the heart center or center of the soul. The final layer, if reached, will explain the true nature of the spirit, the reason for their life, the lessons trying to be learned, and what the soul needs for further ascension. This innermost layer connects us to our internal journey as a soul through many lifetimes and reminds us to not be as judgmental on any spirit for mistakes made in one life.

Counseling

Now that we're more aware of the spirit's reasoning for being earthbound, it's now time to work though the layers of energy to release heavy blocks or imprints. The blocks and imprints of energy are the reasons the spirit is heavier and more grounded than other spirits. By lifting or removing them, spirits have a different sense of awareness and a more positive view of the transition process. Usually, counseling can be conducted in several ways depending on the circumstances. The type of counseling we do isn't compared to psychiatric or psychological counseling. That is something you should try to stay away from, unless you have a specialized degree. The type of counseling we do is more of advice, support, encouragement, and message work. In the end, many spirits simply want to be heard before moving on.

The bulk of your counseling or support will be through the outermost layers regarding more recent events. Emotional and mental support will be needed to help the spirit release their hold on the physical world. What type of emotions is the spirit going through? How do they feel about their passing, and why can't they let go? Every situation is going to be different, so you're going to have to try several different ways to help the spirit move on.

Things to think about when trying to counsel or support earthbound spirits are:

Does the spirit need counseling or support or do they just need someone to guide them to the light?

Sometimes they are completely aware of their death and just have no idea where to go. I know it's hard to imagine this because we can't fathom the idea of someone getting lost on the way into the light. The truth is they don't get lost; it's their perception and awareness that may shield them from the guiding light. They are essentially blind to it. You may just need to change their focus into the higher spiritual planes or bring in a guide from the other side to help with the transition. If you find that the spirit is not open or receptive to counseling or guidance, you may need to come back at a different time. Spirits, just like the living, need to be in the mood for help. Try to ask your guides to help you monitor the spirit and key you in when the earthbound spirit might be more willing to listen.

How receptive is the spirit to help if they do need support?

Emotions can cloud the spirit's perception making them very difficult to help. Greed, jealousy, lust, anger, or envy are just some of the emotions that can create illusions to the spirit. Quite often the only thing they need or want is the same thing keeping them from crossing. A good analogy is an anchor with the physical world holding them to the physical life they once had. By helping the spirit let go of these addictions or cravings, you can help them achieve a sense of freedom from the pain. Again, try to stay away from psychological counseling unless you have a degree or form of training. Comparing some of your personal stories with the spirit's situation can sometimes be enough. Showing them ways to let go and move on will be helpful.

Are there any other spirits around influencing their awareness, and will they impact the spirit's judgment?

Earthbound spirits that are held captive by fear of other lower-level spirits may hinder the spirit from listening to you. This would be considered a hostage situation by a lower-level entity. Though the earthbound spirit may seem very willing to listen to the entity and work with it, you need to remember that this is only because the earthbound spirit has been manipulated by the entity. You will learn that by removing or clearing the negative influence first with the help of spiritual protectors, you can gain the trust and acceptance from the victimized earthbound spirit. This can be done through clearing techniques and imprint removal of the entity. Just like you would remove entities from physical people, you can remove entities from earthbound spirits. It's a double-edged sword when dealing with this issue. In order to obtain trust by the spirit, you must remove the entity. In order to remove the entity, you must gain the willingness of the earthbound spirit. You'll have to work this situation slowly and carefully. The earthbound spirit's guides will help with clearing work as you work with your guides.

Do they feel comfortable receiving this support from you, or does it need to come from someone else?

Just because we can hear, see, and feel spirits, doesn't mean we're the best choice for counseling for the spirits. There will be times you need to call in help from others around you that may have a better support system for the earthbound spirit. Not all situations can be handled by a friendly chat or counseling. A spirit's needs may go deeper. Spirits may need deeds to be completed on the physical plane in order to move into the light. If the spirit needs a blessing from a priest or clergyman to know that they will be accepted into heaven, then you would need to seek out assistance to help the spirit get what they need. If a warrior spirit needs a certain ceremony to be performed in order to move into the spirit world, you'll need to seek out the proper assistance to perform this act. Having connections to these types of services will help you in your rescue work. Every time you experience a new situation that calls for professional assistance, document the referral and keep record of it for future use.

Do spirits need messages sent to their loved ones?

Becoming the messenger can be very important to spirits that felt they couldn't express themselves at the end of their life. Saying goodbye, telling someone they love them, giving a friend advice, helping a family member out in a time of need, etc., will be beneficial to the earthbound spirit so that they can find peace in their transition. Locating the recipient to the message might not be so easy. If the spirit doesn't help you find the recipient directly, you could spend countless hours searching for them. Coming up with a message blog or chat group for messages may be beneficial. As long as the spirit knows that the message is getting sent out to the community, it could be enough for them to let go and move on. Try to keep messages that are very personal to the spirit private, and seek out the recipient directly if possible. There are times when spirits want to send messages to people who have already moved into spirit. If this occurs, the recipient in spirit will often appear to you. Connect the two spirits together for communication and healing. The recipient in spirit will usually help the earthbound spirit transition once the message is heard and the earthbound spirit is appeased.

Shedding the Layers

By working through the emotional, mental, and karmic issues the spirit is facing, you help remove the imprints that affect the spirit's vibration. Each time you help the spirit work through something that is holding them back, the imprint of that emotion or thought gets released, making the spirit lighter. In turn by helping the spirit become lighter, you help raise the spirit's vibration, linking them into a higher state of awareness. This new state of awareness changes their perspective to their transition and connects them with their spiritual friends and family on the other side.

To remove the heavy layers of energy, I imagine the energy like a thick, heavy blanket on the spirit. When we connect with a situation the spirit overcomes or lets go of, I imagine this imprint floating away from the layer of energy. I'll sometimes imagine clearing the imprint away myself by pushing the imprint off the energy, like you're clearing away dirt off someone's shirt. This visualization helps dissipate the energy being removed so that it isn't hovering above the spirit like dust or residue. You want to clear away and shield the spirit from the residual energy you are removing by neutralizing it or dissipating it. I work with angelic helpers that remove energy blocks and residual imprints when they are removed from spirits. These angelic clearers take the energy away to be used for the highest and best within the world or universe.

Each time you remove an imprint, the layer of energy changes. You may notice changes through feelings, colors, or images the spirit sends out. The energy around the spirit will change, too. You may notice subtle changes in the energy of the room, feelings from other spirits on the other side may become more excited or energized, or environmental changes may occur. Everything will indicate that the earthbound spirit's vibration is elevating to a more positive and lighter vibration. Once you have a feeling that the spirit is ready to move on, you prepare for the spirit's transition.

Guidance

Helping the Spirit Transition

There are several ways to help the spirit cross into the light. It's all going to depend on what the spirit's needs are. Not all spirits can make the transition the same way. You will notice some spirits find moving into the light to be a very natural experience, while other spirits need a little extra support to walk them through the spiritual door. While you may have removed blocks or imprints from the spirit's energy, making them more receptive to the light, they still may need a gentle nudge from guides, angels, family, or friends from the spiritual planes. There are three common ways that I help spirits transition during a direct rescue, depending on the situation.

Opening up a door to the spiritual world.
Just like when you visualize closing a spiritual door, you can also visualize yourself opening a spiritual door. You just need to imply the right energy vibration through thought and intent. This spiritual door's intent is to bring in the white light of divine energy and build a vortex to the spiritual world. The door will often be accompanied by a guide or shepherding spirit so that the spirit has a guide to help them walk through. My spiritual door opens to the right of me, while clearing residual energy moves to the left of me. In time, you're going to figure out what flow of energy works for you through trial and error. Not everyone's visualization is going to work the same way. The flow of energy I work with presented itself to me through my gut instincts and through manifesting exactly how it wanted to. So when I open a spiritual door, it presents itself to my right, just above my shoulder with a very bright light. Often the shepherding spirits I work with will open the door once they read my thoughts and understand that the spirit is ready to move on. The earthbound spirits that are ready to go will gently cross and move through the door without restraint. They will usually thank me as they go, and a soft, loving energy transfer will happen between the earthbound spirit and myself.

Bringing a loved one in from the otherside.
Not all spirits can handle the transition easily. A number of spirits will experience more anxiety, fear, or uncertainty of the spiritual door. Even though they know it's their time and have removed the blocks keeping them earthbound, the spirit can still become scared as they prepare for their journey. This is when calling in extra guidance from the spiritual side will be beneficial. I'll usually link in with the spirit world and ask who is standing by to assist the earthbound spirit. The spirit world loves helping in a spirit's transition and will almost always be

standing by to guide the way. You may even have a large number of family members waiting to help walk the spirit through. The more spirit energy that comes in to help, the better. As a courtesy, remember to ask the earthbound spirit if the spiritual help coming through is okay. There are times when a spirit steps in to guide an earthbound spirit and the earthbound spirit feels uncomfortable with them being around. So always ask the earthbound spirit if they are comfortable with the spiritual help standing by to help.

Connecting an earthbound spirit to their guide or angel.
Our guides are always by our side—from the moment of our birth until our final transition back into the spiritual world. Even though the earthbound spirit can't sense them, they are always around, watching and supporting the earthbound spirit. By becoming the mediator between the two and linking them back together, the spirit guide can then help the spirit transition through healing, love, and guidance. Guides and angels will present themselves usually through a very loving bright light that manifests in the room when the spirit is preparing for the transition. When you focus your attention to the higher spiritual energy of the guide or angel, the earthbound spirit will follow your lead and focus on the energy as well. This links the earthbound spirit to their guide. Remember that energy flows like a river. The focus of the earthbound spirit moves in a direction parallel to their vibrational flow. By changing the flow to an upward movement toward the guide, the spirit can then connect with them and make contact. There might be a brief moment of introduction between the spirit and their guide, so try not to rush the encounter. Hesitation doesn't always mean trouble. Patience and support will be your best form of guidance.

Specialized Styles of Direct Rescue

We've discussed ways to communicate, counsel, and guide earthbound spirits through direct rescue, usually through the connection to one or two spirits. There are a few different scenarios that may influence the way you complete your rescue with the earthbound spirit. It usually has to do with the environment or situation the spirit is in. Not all rescues are going to occur in a house, building, or traditional paranormal setting. There may be times you'll get called out to a scene of a tragic event or serious accident. You'll need to work through these situations with extra techniques and guidance. Having more than one medium on site may also be beneficial. Oftentimes mediums will have a clearing specialist that works with them during these situations. Other forms of rescues that require more specialized care include, but are not limited to: scene, crisis, group, and hostage.

Scene Rescue

As stated in the chapter of residual energy, spirits can become lost or trapped in an environment created by a residual energy imprint. Usually the impact of the death or time of death gets trapped in the residual imprint that plays over and over again for the spirit to experience. This can also be thought of as a time placement gap where a spirit can become trapped. The best analogy for this would be a battleground like the beaches of Normandy or Pearl Harbor. If a person loses their life during battle, the moment of death can remain trapped in an energy imprint that not only holds the energy of the earthbound spirit but the surrounding environment as well. In this imprint the battle can be relived over and over again. The spirit can't escape the imprisoned environment because they have no recollection of time or their death. We're still trying to figure out exactly why this happens. There are those who think that the time placement occurs through the merger of the spiritual death, change of vibrational frequency, and surrounding influence of the situation.

Since the time of death happened at the same time the residual imprint was formed, the spirit can get caught in the imprint, shielding them from the white light like a cocoon. The created imprint now becomes the only environment the spirit knows. A world unto itself. In order for you to get through to the spirit, you must break down the residual imprint through residual clearing techniques. It is only then can you "wake" the spirit from their dream. It's best to clear the energy slowly so that you don't jolt the spirit out or make them anxious. Often spirits may be trapped in a residual imprint for a long time, so seeing someone from a different time period may be difficult for the spirit to comprehend at first. Allow the residual energy to dissipate slowly like fog clearing under the sun, while slowly moving closer to the spirit's energy. Once the spirit knows that you are there, you can try to start communicating with them. Note, if the spirit isn't receptive to your connection, they can strengthen the residual imprint through their own intent, shielding you and the white light further. So don't be surprised if you need to come back a few times and try again and again to make contact. Every time you touch in with the spirit, you transfer energy to them, enlightening them to their situation. With patience, it does get easier each time you try.

Crisis Rescue

Crisis rescues usually occur during situations involving several people. This would be serious events like plane crashes, hostage situations, terrorist attacks, natural disasters, or anything else that happens suddenly or severely enough to create a crisis-like situation. These crisis situations can confuse people as they can become blindsided. Their death can occur so quickly, they do not realize they are dead. The impact of the situation is too hard for the mind to face; therefore, the spirit creates a false environment that their mind can handle. Think of it like hiding in memory or thought that creates a peaceful situation for the spirit to be in—a form of spiritual denial. The mind of a spirit can create a barrier around them, allowing them to only see what they want to see. They may not even be aware of the other spirits around them if they can't handle the thought of being dead. I'll usually call in several shepherding spirits to help assist in this kind of rescue. The job of the rescue medium is to connect the earthbound spirit to their spiritual guides and angels waiting to guide them. We must merge into their mind and bring them back out. Remember that this must be handled slowly as not to cause more anxiety to the spirit.

There are times during a crisis rescue that all the spirits realize that they have died, and still do not know where to go. The chaos of the situation may hinder the spirits' perception of the white light. There can be spirits that get lost in the confusion and hostility of the event. Think of it like getting lost in a fog of energy. Negative energy pertaining to an event can cause a residual imprint that blocks the spirits from shepherding spirits. Taking care of as many spirits at once will help, though they may need to connect with specialized angels and guides to help them through the tragic situation. Keeping the earthbound spirit calm will be best during this time. Think of it like counseling someone through an emergency situation. When they are calm and clear minded, they can become more receptive to spiritual help and guidance.

Group Rescue

Group rescue isn't the same as a crisis rescue. This type of rescue would be considered more like a gathering of spirits all in one area. Like energy attracts like energy. Spirits will be drawn to each other for comfort and security. You may come into a situation at a sacred site or spiritual historical site where earthbound spirits have grouped together to try to find their way into the light. Your job as a rescue medium is to connect to the spirits as a group and become a mediator between the spirits and shepherding angels coming in to pave the way into the light. These spirits, just like many others, can't see these shepherding spirits because they carry a lower group vibration. A cluster of energy doesn't change unless they all change together. Helping the spirits raise their vibration as a group to see the light will be the best choice during these times as well as connecting them with spiritual guides. Don't be surprised if one or two spirits stay behind a bit longer. Just because spirits cluster together, doesn't mean they will all be ready to go at the same time. Connecting the group to the spiritual guides should be enough for those remaining spirits to have someone to talk to for a while to prepare for their transition.

Hostage

As we observed how earthbound spirits can become hostages to entities attached to them, you will learn that earthbound spirits can also become hostages to other earthbound spirits. These situations normally occur when someone has an attachment of an earthbound spirit around them before death and, after death, become drawn into the captor's vibration and trapped. The captor's energy can be dense and dark enough to shield the white light from the transitioning spirit's view, making them scared, lost, and confused. Many victims to abusers can get caught in this situation as well. Murder suicides are the most common type of hostage situation. Unless the victim in spirit can connect with angelic forces quickly enough, the abuser has the chance to overshadow the white light and trap the victim in their vibration. I've personally seen a fair number of hostage situations with spirits, and the victim rarely feels strong or brave enough to break free from the abuser's grasp. It's the position of the rescue medium to act as a clearer first to remove the abuser's energy from the victimized earthbound spirit. Sometimes finding a way to get the abuser's attention long enough to clear a large enough gap between the victim and the abuser might work. Finding a way to bring in a transitionary guide and angel for the victim to quickly move them into the light when they detach will be helpful. Once the victimized spirit has made the transition, you can start working on helping the abuser to transition or clear them from the area. Spirit police or guards may arrive and form a barrier between the abuser and the medium to make sure the medium isn't at risk of being attacked. If the free will of the medium is compromised, the spirit police or guards will remove the abusing spirit and take them to a holding area in the spiritual realm for healing and guidance.

CHAPTER THIRTEEN

Indirect Rescue

Our second form of rescue comes through indirect techniques. You're not going to have as much contact with spirits compared with direct rescue, but it does serve a purpose for spirits at a distance. There have been several occasions when I've had people contact me from all over the world asking me to clear spirits from their homes or to clear spirit attachments. The biggest question people ask me is how can this be done from a distance? When you understand how energy works, you can get a better sense of how distant rescue or indirect rescue can be performed.

Indirect rescue is a form of rescue that is completed from a distance or through an indirect energy link when you and the spirit exchange an energy transfer through prayers, affirmations, and remote viewing. Indirect rescue can also be performed in an indirect rescue circle where you try to connect to spirits at a distance, pull in their energy, and communicate with them. The link between medium and spirit isn't as strong as direct rescue, but it can be effective when the spirit is receptive to help.

There are three ways that I believe indirect rescue can be performed. They are:

1. Prayers and affirmations,
2. Remote viewing and linking with spirit indirectly, and
3. Bringing in earthbound spirit energy through thought and intent.

Prayers and Affirmations

Prayers and affirmations are a great way to send energy out to earthbound spirits. It's a way to help raise the energy vibration around the earthbound spirit and connect them with a new awareness of their situation. If you concentrate long enough on any subject that you are praying about, the energy eventually finds its way to the recipient. You don't need to know who the spirit is, where they are, what they are going through, or how to help them cross. Just the act of sending prayers and affirmations to the spirit can help lift their constant vibration, bridging the gap between the earthbound plane and the spiritual plane. Once the spirit raises their vibration high enough, their awareness changes, connecting them to the white light and their spirit guides.

There are countless prayers to help spirits transition into the light. You can use any prayers you find online, in books, or just make up your own. Try to find a prayer that concentrates on removing blocks, relieving their fears, linking them to family and friends on the other side, and finding peace within the white light. There aren't any common prayers that all mediums use; most are borrowed from other mediums that help spirits cross over. You're welcome to use the prayer that I often use for any spirit that needs help finding their way. The prayer is called *Light the Way*:

Dear Lord, I pray for those who are in need of hope, strength, and encouragement in the spirit world. May the grace of your love shield them from fear, comfort them in sadness, and lift their minds from darkness. Surround these earthbound spirits with healing and compassion in your holy name, and light the way to everlasting peace. Amen.

Affirmations are a wonderful tool to use to help earthbound spirits gain strength, receive hope, and calm fears during their transition. You don't need to know exactly who the spirit is or where they are in order to help them. Sending out energy that encourages a spirit to heal and feel comforted is very helpful and does aid in their rescue in an indirect way. Even though you don't know where to send the energy to, the flow of energy will lead directly to where it is needed. It's sort of like the magnet effect. If a spirit is in need of comfort and security, then an affirmation that aids in comfort will find its opposite vibration. Another analogy is to think of medicine. You can't always direct the medicine you take to go into a certain part of your body, though it always finds a way to help the area in need. The energy will find its way to be helpful to the earthbound spirit. Certain affirmations that I use to help aid in a spirit's transition are:

- Let your heart be your guide.
- May the wandering spirit find their way into the light.
- Let there be light in the darkness for those who are in need.
- May the love of the angels guide these spirits home.
- May earthbound spirits be comforted and shielded from pain.
- Let there be peace in the mind and heart of the wounded spirit.

Remote Viewing

Remote viewing is a psychic link between you and the earthbound spirit through a distance. In psychic and mediumship development, you might have learned about the form of linking in with an object, place, or person through remote viewing. Remote viewing is seeing or sensing the spirit at a distance through your mediumship and ESP abilities. You can link up to the energy of the object, place, or person by connecting to some aspect of them, like a name. For example, if someone were to tell you that they had an earthbound spirit in their home in Ireland and needed you to help clear the spirit from their house, but you lived in Australia, you would need to link in with the spirit through remote viewing. By connecting to the energy of the house in Ireland, you can set up a direct link of energy between you and the area. Once the link is made, you can read the energy of the area, including the spirits that are in the house. This is how to connect and communicate with the earthbound spirit at a distance. The link isn't as strong as a direct rescue, but it can still be useful to aid in the transition.

I had conducted an indirect rescue with a spirit in Scotland while I was still in the United States. The woman gave me her name and the town's name. That was enough to link with her and her home. From there, I was able to sense other energies in the home, such as other family members, animals, surrounding objects and neighbors, residual energy of the house, and any spirits that were in the area. Through this link, I was able to connect to the earthbound spirits she needed help with. The owner of the house explained to me that she needed three spirits to be released from her mother. Her mother had taken ill about ten years ago with a high temperature when the spirits attached to her. They had the sense that there were three spirits: one man and two women. They were verbally very abusive to her and kept her awake at night. Her mother felt the spirits with her all the time. They had various mediums working with her mother, but unfortunately, the spirits still remained with her. I told the owner that I would look into the situation and connect to the spirits during one of my spirit rescue classes to help train my students. She thanked me and I told her I would email her with details once they became available.

During class, I explained to the students the situation and we conducted an indirect rescue circle to connect to the spirits that were attached to the mother in Scotland. We linked up with the woman's name and town in Scotland and brought in the energy of the three spirits. Two of the three spirits were not hostile or dangerous. The first earthbound spirit was a man who had lived in the area, passed away, stayed earthbound, and wandered around with other earthbound spirits in the area. In his life, he passed from a heart condition in his mid fifties and lived alone in the area. He had a beard and shaggy hair. He felt like he could have been a caretaker or farmer in the area since he had a great deal of knowledge of fixing things and tinkering with objects. He showed us farm animals, large areas of land, and farming tools. He seemed to have lived around the time period of the 1920s to 1940s. He had a quiet and gentle energy but seemed very tired and weary of his situation. He wasn't looking to engage in any physical or abusive behavior, rather he was just connected to the other earthbound spirits. The class was able to help him disconnect from the other women and help him cross into the light by bringing in one of his spirit family members. He seemed fairly relieved of his situation and thanked us for helping him.

The second spirit was that of a woman in her late seventies, tall and thin, with gray hair pulled back. She seemed very strong-willed and intelligent. She also seemed to have the nature of a caretaker. She explained that she was a family member of the sick mother. She had stayed behind in death to make sure the woman was taken care of and not alone. She seemed to have been someone who was very protective and would not leave her side.

It seemed to the class and me that she was more than ready to disconnect from the sick mother. But how did she gain all of these earthbound spirits when she was sick and two of the three had no interest in her? That would lead us to the third earthbound spirit who seemed to be controlling the whole situation.

The third spirit was a woman in her sixties who was overweight and passed from many illnesses, mostly breathing issues. She was very emotionally and mentally unstable and seemed to have been that way most of her life. She told us that she had been extremely unhappy and very lonely since childhood. She was abused as a child from both her parents and only received love or comfort when she would take ill. That formed an emotional imprint on her that compelled her to be sick often so that she could feel loved from others. This carried on through her adult life. When speaking to the woman who was earthbound, she became very upset and started to cry. Her pain and suffering from the lack of love and support of her family was too much to handle. She wanted to be free from the pain but wasn't sure how to let go.

The reason the mother in Scotland became sick all the time was because the earthbound spirit wanted the mother to get sick. The earthbound spirit could experience comfort and healing all over again through the mother. She didn't seem to care what she was doing to all the people involved; she only wanted to relieve her pain and emotional wounds the only way she knew how. By helping the earthbound spirit understand that the love and comfort she was longing for was in the light waiting for her, she was able to release her hold on the sick mother and move on into the spirit world. It did take time for the earthbound spirit to believe us and understand that love was waiting for her on the other side. She didn't seem to think that anyone in spirit would love her enough to accept her. She never felt loved by her parents that were on the other side. So, naturally she felt hesitant to move on. The class and I brought in the energy of her guardian angel to surround her with love and healing. The angel's energy was strong enough to help the earthbound spirit understand that she would be supported on the other side and quickly moved into the light with the angel. The sick mother was able to be released from all three spirits, relieving her of her illnesses associated with the spirits.

Bringing in an Earthbound Spirit

You don't always need to know who or where the earthbound spirit is. Just allowing your thought and intent to lead the way should be enough. This can be related to the same principle of attracting like energy to like energy. If you set your intent to link up with earthbound spirits, the energy will flow and find an earthbound spirit, linking it with you. This too can be done at a distance. The link between you and spirit should have enough of a connection to communicate with them. Once the link is made, the energy of the earthbound spirit can come in.

This isn't the easiest way to find spirits, nor is it the safest. I rarely call in earthbound spirits that are unfamiliar to me or ones I have no background information on. You never know who you're going to connect with. It's best to make sure you have your spiritual team ready to assist you if you should call in spirits to help them. Most of the time when I call in earthbound spirits, I'll usually think about situations that may have occurred such as natural disasters, terrorist attacks, plane crashes, or any other world/national occurrences that may have resulted in many deaths. A number of the spirits may have been hesitant to move on, as we know not everyone is ready to go at the same time. I'll call in any spirits left behind during these times to see if our assistance is needed.

Do know that when you call in spirits from these disaster situations, it might be best to have a few mediums linking with the energy so that you do not get overwhelmed. Plus, it's easier to have several opinions from other mediums to help validate the information coming through. This is when I recommend calling spirits in through an indirect rescue circle.

Indirect Rescue Circle

An indirect rescue circle is a great resource to help connect with earthbound spirits with the assistance of other rescue mediums. It gives you the chance to have a controlled environment with earthbound spirits with the help of not only other mediums, but also the spiritual teams of other mediums, too. You could literally fill the whole room with protection and spiritual help with guides, angels, protectors, healers, clearers, gatekeepers, family members in spirit, and animal guides from all the mediums in the room. So having this type of environment during a rescue is not only beneficial to the spirit, but beneficial to you as well. Setting up an indirect rescue circle takes some serious thought and consideration. You're not going to want to just get together for a party and decide to do a rescue at the last minute with a few friends. It's going to take a bit more planning and protection than that. Things I would consider preparing in advance for an indirect rescue circle are:

Place and Time
Where do you plan on having this circle group? Again, I wouldn't recommend your home as this is a sacred space that should be honored as a no fly zone so that you maintain your sanity. I would choose a psychic center, spiritualist church, outdoor area that is spiritual in nature, or a meeting area where you feel safe. The time should be when everyone in your group is free from distractions of everyday life. Make sure the area you are in doesn't have time restrictions. I would hate to see you kicked out of a public area in the middle of a rescue, so try to be properly prepared.

Spiritual Tools
Protection and clearing tools should be used if you have them on hand. Crystals, salt, singing bowls, smudging, or any other tool to help prepare the area and clear it after the rescue is recommended. Sometimes I light a few candles for intent to help prepare the energy of the room. It also gives the earthbound spirits notice that we are getting prepared to communicate with them.

Bring in Spiritual Help
You should never do rescue work without your spiritual team. Call in your guides, angels, gatekeepers, protectors, healers, clearers, and animal totems for assistance. You may also feel the energy of shepherding spirits or teams from the other side coming in to help as well. I'll usually ask for angels to stand on all four corners of the room to help stabilize the energy and ask our guides to form a circle of protection around the group.

Shielding Yourself and the Circle
Setting up your white light shield or protective shield around your energy is needed. Calling in your spiritual team is wonderful, but you're also responsible for your own protection as well. I'll set up my shield and expand it around everyone in the group. If everyone does that, then the protection circle should be strong. This doesn't keep earthbound spirits away, it only sets your thought and intent that you don't plan on becoming the victim of an earthbound spirit.

Calling in the Spirits

This is when you would call out to spirits directly relating to an event in the area or around the world that you feel might have resulted in an earthbound spirit. Recent events in the news might provoke the need for an indirect rescue circle. You can link your energy to the event that occurred and ask any spirits connected to that event to come into your circle.

Once you've made contact with the spirit and have communicated with them to find out details, you can begin your rescue work to see if they are ready to move on. You would follow the same steps to help counsel them through their issues and help remove blocks as in a direct rescue. Once they are ready to move on, open up the spiritual door to the other side and call in family, friends, guides, or angels to walk them through.

You may have your own technique for rescue as you develop your own style over time. That's fine as long as the spirit gets what they need. Follow your instincts and always ask for help from your guides and angels. When you've completed the rescue circle, remember to clear yourself, others in the group, and all residual energy left in the space. Thank your spiritual team for coming in and shut down mediumistically so that earthbound spirits do not follow you home. (Hopefully).

CHAPTER FOURTEEN

Spirit Attachments

Spirit rescue can be confusing, as we are required to handle several responsibilities or situations that pertain to earthbound spirits, including rescue, clearing, and attachment removal. People know rescue mediums help earthbound spirits into the light, but not all circumstances will require a rescue of an earthbound spirit. There are those who might need a more forceful approach. This is where rescue mediums switch to being clearers instead of rescuers. As we discussed before, one of the main roles of a rescue medium is to clear earthbound spirits from people, places, or objects when they become harmful. Before I go into detail about how to remove earthbound spirits, we should discuss what types of spirits attach to people and why.

Not So Negative Spirit Attachment

It can be said most spirit attachments actually come from earthbound spirits— spirits that are just looking to find security and comfort from a living person when they become lost, scared, confused, or worn out from wandering. They look for people who remind them of someone they know or anyone with similar energy to themselves to make them feel comforted. We need to examine why spirits attach to us in order to understand how to remove them. Though most attachments aren't harmful to people, they can be very draining on the energy of the host. Removing spirit attachments isn't just beneficial to the person experiencing the attachment, but also to the spirit so they can continue on with their spiritual journey. To make it easier to understand, I've listed a few scenarios that explain why spirits may attach and why they are a little less threatening in nature. They are:

The Clinger

Not all spirits are going to be comfortable with their new energy in spirit. Spirits can get very anxious and miss their physical body. They may search out and find someone who was like them or someone they can relate to, to attach to.

This helps them connect back in with a life force and makes them feel comforted with familiar feelings of being grounded into a physical body. There isn't any personal connection to the person, rather they just need your body to feel alive again. These types of attachments happen more frequently than people realize, and these spirits rarely stay for very long.

They Like Your Energy

Earthbound spirits that wander around searching for the white light can get stuck or fixed in an area because they have no direction or stimulation to guide them. People here in the physical world with high vibrations will sometimes draw in these spirits like a magnet because the spirits think that this person might guide them or help them in some way. Those in the healing profession give off a certain vibration that signals to spirits that they are someone the spirit can trust and receive healing from. Meanwhile people in the psychic and spiritual fields radiate a light much brighter than others, so it's only natural for earthbound spirits to be attracted to them. Just being in the right place at the wrong time can make you vulnerable to an attachment. Removal of these attachments are easier than others as most of these spirits are looking for a higher vibration to merge with. Once they get sight of the white light, they quickly detach, moving on to transition.

They Think You're Someone They Know

A great deal of earthbound spirits will search out people who either remind them of someone they were close to, or they literally think you are that person and stick to you like glue. Loss of relationships or heartbreaks can cause spirits to be very vulnerable, making them very anxious and lonely. If you remind them of someone they once loved, they could attach to feel comforted by you. Removal of these types of attachments can take time as you need to remind the spirit that the host is not the person they think they are. Confusion and illusion will be strong with this type of attachment. Once the spirit can let go of the person they long for, they detach to move on.

Children Searching for a Parental Role Model
The children that temporarily become earthbound due to emotional and mental trauma may wander until they find someone with strong parental energy that they feel comfortable with. If you're a mom or dad who has strong nurturing energy, earthbound children may find their way to you for security and assistance. Attaching to you is more of a protective instinct. You become their security blanket when they are lost or confused. Removal of these attachments is very easy once you're able to bring in a spiritual family member from the other side

or an angelic guide for the spirit child to follow. There will be times you have to remind the host that they too need to let go of the child attachment. People can feel the need to keep the child safe within them. By sheltering and protecting this child in their energy, they feel they are keeping the spirit child from harm. Your responsibility is to remind the host that by letting the child go and helping them move on, the child would be much happier and well protected.

Spirits that Are Trying to Hide

Spirits who aren't ready to move into the light will hide in the energy of someone else, thinking this will shield them or camouflage them from their guides and angels. They know it's their time to go, but for personal reasons, decide to stay behind and hide in the host of someone who has very similar qualities or traits. This doesn't work, even though they think it does. Guides and angels are always aware of their whereabouts, so this game of hide and seek doesn't last long. Guides can't force a spirit to cross, but they do continue to encourage the transition on occasion. Hiding in the energy of another person only delays the inevitable. Once they realize that, they release their grip on the person and make their transition.

Negative Attachments

The most common forms of spirit attachments that we hear about in the media or in traditional spooky ghost stories are those earthbound spirits out for ill intent or have negative agendas. People are usually more aware of these types of attachments because they interfere with the physical host more often than those looking for comfort. It's easy to think that only negative or evil spirits will attach to people to harm or harass people in the physical world. The world itself is filled with negative people who look for unsuspecting victims, so why would the spirit world be any different? The truth is, it's not. There are many spirits out in the lower levels of the spiritual world that still search out people who would make easy targets or victims to harass. To be sure, there are a great many negative spirits out there, but there are also a lot of angels and spiritual warriors to keep us safe from lower-level spirits. So, the lower-level attachments are not as common as you might think they are because of this spiritual protection. The types of earthbound spirits that attach for negative reasons would be:

Those with Addictive Behaviors

Earthbound spirits that aren't ready to give up their physical addictions may search out someone with similar addictions, making the person in the physical world more vulnerable than they were before. These earthbound spirits can influence the host to crave the addictive substance or situation more often so that they can experience it themselves again through the host. This can lead to a long and stressful life for the person with the attachment. Any chance of removing the addictive behavior has been compromised, making the host more likely to continue the addictive behavior until the spirit releases. Addictions can lead to mental disorders, sickness, and death. Once the host is no longer able to serve the spirit, they move on to find another host to satisfy their needs. Removal of these attachments requires help from healers, guides, protectors, and angels from the other side. Strong protective shields must be secured around you and everyone involved. Most often these spirit attachments require forceful removal from the host, so be prepared for a struggle. The type of spirit attachments that require less of a forceful approach are ones that are looking for healing themselves. Counseling and support from you and others will help the spirit release their hold on the victim.

Sexual Tendencies

Earthbound spirits with severe sexual addictions will often search out the opposite sex to attach to for sexual stimulation and manipulation. These types of attachments can actually force themselves onto the host in a sexual way, forcing the host to experience a sexual exchange. Penetration and sexual touching is very common for these spirits. People burdened with these attachments feel trapped in a sexually abusive relationship with no way to remove the abuser. Typically, most of these attachments will release their victims quickly once you bring in your spiritual clearing team. They instinctively know that these spiritual clearers will take them to a healing area that will try to remove the sexual addictions. By leaving quickly, they move to another host to continue the sexual torment. Unfortunately, you cannot have the spiritual protectors hold the spirit back from harming other people. This compromises the will of the spirit. Until they start harming others there's nothing you can do. It's similar to here in the physical world. You know someone is a sexual predator, but can't do anything about it until the police catch them in the act. The same rules apply in the spirit world.

Abusers

Those in the physical world who search out victims to abuse will usually continue their abusive tendencies even after death. The need to control and victimize other people becomes a conditioned behavior, which becomes a strong imprint in the personality of the earthbound spirit. Spirits who stay clear of the white light during transition due to fear of judgement will quite often become angry, feeding into their need to hurt others. As a general rule, spirit abusers have no desire to move on and will continue to jump from host to host until the anger of the spirit dissipates. Abusers take on many forms from the emotional, physical, sexual, mental, or karmic. Bringing in your protection and clearing spiritual team will be needed for these removals.

Abusers with Family Cords

Abusive spirits can stay within the same family through generations, abusing one family member at a time. For example, they may attach on to a child to feed off their energy, then jump from one child to the next every time a child grows to an adult. This can last for generations. There have been several accounts of abusing spirits that wait for someone to be reincarnated, just to attach to them again and start the abuse all over. This would be in the form of a karmic abuse situation. Cords of connection to the abused victims and all family members usually need to be severed and the spirit attachment removed from all blood lines.

Mentally Unstable

Even though we shed our physical bodies after death and move into a lighter spiritual vibration, our minds still carry imprints or memories from our life. Any mental disorders that the physical form endured may carry on into the spiritual mind. The mental handicap could be strong enough to hinder the transition of the spirit, making them earthbound. These spirits may wander due to fear or anxiety from their death. They will usually search out hosts to feed off their energy, thinking they will become healthy through the mind of someone else. There are cases where the mental instability of the earthbound spirit makes them do things they don't even realize is bad until the host gets hurt. The mental disorder usually carries a very low vibration holding the spirit back from the white light. By helping the spirit disconnect from their mental condition, you help the spirit raise their vibration. This is usually done by the removal of imprints within the spiritual mind. I wouldn't get too involved with this without strict guidance and leadership of your spiritual team. This should always be done as a last resort. Messing around with the mind imprints of spirits can be very damaging. Usually spiritual clearers and healers will come in to help remove the spirit attachment. This is much safer for both the spirit and the host.

Where Attachments Latch On

As discussed before, our auras need to be strong and vibrant in order to ward off attachments. If your aura is weakened in certain spots, spirits can penetrate through these openings in your aura and attach onto your energy and chakras.

Once they get inside your chakras, they start influencing you emotionally, mentally, and physically. There are common areas in your aura that get weakened or damaged the most. This is where we "dump" our baggage energetically so that we don't have to deal with them at the current moment. These dumping grounds that we put heavy and dense energy will weaken the aura, leaving it vulnerable for attack. Other areas on our body are more vulnerable to spirit attack depending on how low the vibration is around that site. Listed below are the most common areas in our body that allow for attachments to latch on.

Back of the Head

Earthbound spirits will generally stand behind someone rather than out in front. This is a way to hide from the medium or person in order to watch them or just hang onto their energy for comfort. By doing this their heavy energy can influence our aura, lowering it and weakening it. A good analogy would be like having a heavy weight placed on your aura. Over time, your aura becomes tired and starts to break down. Learning proper shielding will keep earthbound spirits off your aura. For those in the spiritual or psychic communities, while developing and stimulating chakras, the chakra in the back of the head becomes stimulated and awakened as well. This is the Bindu chakra. It relates to health and vitality. It sits in the back of your head, just above the neck. Those who work in the spiritual and healing fields may notice pressure or stimulated energy in the back of the head while working. This is due to the Bindu chakra working and sending out energy to the rest of your body. Spirits that are looking to attack you will often go straight for this chakra first to lower your energy and disconnect you from a harmonious energy flow. Once this area is under attack, the rest of your aura can become compromised. Again, this is when you need to strengthen your energy and form a shield of protection around your head. Asking earthbound spirits to back off a little can help as well. Learning how to set up your personal space between you and spirit is essential.

Back of the Neck and Shoulders

This is where we store much of our stress and anxiety. Think of it like carrying the weight of the world on our shoulders. You technically are when you keep holding onto your heavy emotional and mental problems there. This in turn weakens your aura because of the heavy imprints in your energy. Anytime outside influences lower the vibration of a certain spot on your body, it weakens the surrounding aura. This creates holes or gaps in your aura, making it easier for spirits to penetrate through. Just like we discussed before about energetic layers, you need to work from the inside and go out. You need to remove all imprints and negative energy from your aura. Deep massage to the area and pressure stimulation can help by removing these energetic imprints. Once the imprints are removed, you can strengthen your aura with healing techniques. Once you start feeling a tightness or heaviness around your neck and shoulders, immediately work on removing the negative energy before spirits attach.

Ears

Spirit attackers love going through the ears of their victims. This tactic makes for a quick and easy transfer to the mind. Victims of spirits moving through the ears will often hear noises or voices from the spirit. Feeling pressure around your ears may not always signify you are being attacked by a spirit. High level spirits will also stimulate a pressure-like feeling when they are trying to talk to you. High pitched sounds, tickling, or tingling around the ears are usually a good sign from family and friends in spirit. Feelings of pain or strong pressure inside the ear usually indicate a lower spirit form. Maintaining a white light field around your head should prevent any lower spirit attack. The only energy allowed to come through must resonate as neutral or the same vibration as your white light shield.

Throat

This is a common area for people who have a hard time expressing themselves. The throat chakra becomes compromised due to the lack of communication and stimulation. Through holding in your words and truth, you weaken your throat chakra. The best way to describe the feeling or sensation when your chakra is weakened is by feeling a tightness or pressure around your throat. Lumps in the throat and thyroid problems can manifest physically through a damaged throat chakra. Spirits can attach easily through this site as it is an area of weakness physically. Certain parts of the body are stronger than others depending on how often it is used. The throat area is one of the weakest. Maintaining a strong throat chakra and strong aura around your throat is important.

Chest

Your heart chakra is in the middle of your chest and is one of the first chakras to be compromised when you are suffering through hardships and loss. People who suffered through a broken heart or emotional situation can easily become victims of spirit attachments. Quite often these spirits will have a weakened emotional element of their soul, making them a perfect match for someone with a low vibration. Keeping a strong shield around your aura during times of loss or sadness can help keep spirits off your heart chakra until you feel better.

Gut

This area can either be your weakest spot in your energy or your strongest depending on how much stress you are under, your ability to overcome obstacles, your outlook on life, and your confidence in yourself. The world can be a cruel and harsh place to live, which can put stress on your solar plexus chakra located in the middle of your stomach. Physical symptoms of a weakened solar plexus will include digestive disorders, gall bladder issues, liver disease, leaky gut, excessive weight in your stomach, and rashes. Stomach pain and bloating are very common signs that your energy is being drained and lowered by stress, anxiety, fear, anger, regret, and so on. Quite often, these physical symptoms will persist even when you've eliminated all physical causes when you have an attachment. Spirits will feed off the negative energy in the imprints and will often manifest more damaging physical symptoms to gain strength within your body. By alleviating these emotional and mental issues in your life, you can build and strengthen the energy in your solar plexus, shielding you and your aura from spirit attack.

Sexual Organs

Women especially can host spirit attachments in their uterus and ovaries depending on the type of attachment they have. Attachments that house in this area can often be non-threatening, like small children or wounded women. The female reproductive organs can become a protective shell for spirits to rest in. The life force and nurturing element of the uterus and ovaries can also draw in spirits in need of healing. Those spirits with negative tendencies will bury into the sexual organs to stimulate and abuse their victims sexually. Stimulating the host repeatedly through these sites can lower the vibration of the host, making them most susceptible to attack.

Lower Back

The lower back is very susceptible to spirit attack with people suffering from back pain or lower back issues. Spine pain can be extremely hard on a person, weakening their energy and aura in that area. Pain usually causes a weakened aura due to the negative imprints of the site. Spirits can attach to a person through the lower back when the aura is weakened or damaged. Spirits that are looking to harass or harm someone will usually stimulate more pain in that area, making the victim helpless and vulnerable.

Sites of Surgery or Illness

Places on your body that suffer through illness can damage the aura in that area. Just like back pain, areas in your body that are sick lower the vibration of that site making it susceptible to attack. Spirits will commonly enter sites of recent surgeries as they are not as protected. The body is very susceptible during surgery, so it's best to ask for extra protection from your healers and protectors to stand guard over you while you are in surgery.

Signs of a Spirit Attachment

Now that we're familiar with the types of spirit attachments that are out there and where they can enter our body, it's time to examine how you can tell if someone has an attachment. Not all symptoms will present the same way, and not all of these symptoms mean that someone has an attachment. We have to logically assume that most of these issues will be the result of a mental, emotional, or physical source that initiates within the person themselves. We have to rule out all logical explanations of these symptoms before we start jumping to the conclusion that someone has an attachment. Once all logical and reasonable explanations have been ruled out, you would start conducting a spirit attachment investigation.

Mediums such as myself with strong clairsentient ability will normally feel or sense a spirit attachment right away. Feeling imprints or heavy energy within a person may signify an attachment. Mediums with clairvoyant ability may be able to see or sense the spirit entity on or in a person. So, we're going to be using our ESP and mediumship abilities to investigate the attachment along with examining all symptoms of the victim. For situations when the spirit entity has become so strong that it has taken over the mind, body, and emotions of the victimized host, less investigating is done and more protective, clearing work is initiated. Common symptoms of spirit attachments relating to physical, mental, emotional, and psychological are:

PHYSICAL

Sickness

This would be an ongoing sickness that lingers for a prolonged period of time that doesn't improve. Spirits can hinder the healing ability of the body, making it reject medication to properly heal the illness. Average sicknesses that usually heal quickly can be affected by this. Reoccurring or chronic illness that persists may also indicate an attachment. Abusers of their hosts drain their energy, making them more susceptible to viruses and bacterial infections. Spirits can also feed the illness, creating a more negative environment, so illnesses that get worse right away for no apparent reason can signify an attachment.

Fatigue

Fatigue is by far one of the most common symptoms of spirit attachments. It can be very hard on the body to house two spiritual forms, draining the prana or life force from the body quickly. Spirits that live off the energy of their host quite often will drain the host. This usually indicates that the invading spirit is trying to use the energy of the host to regain strength while trying to heal itself. These type of symptoms must be evaluated by a doctor first to rule out any deficiencies, illnesses, or physical abnormalities before we investigate for an attachment. Regardless of whether the person has an attachment, healing or chakra balancing should probably be performed to help supplement with the doctor's treatments.

Pain

Pain outside the normal wear and tear of our daily lives can be a symptom. Average soreness and digestive upset should be handled normally under the direction of your doctor. Pain that is constant and in one area can indicate a spirit imprint or attachment. Pain is an indicator of spirit attack because the spirit is invading your body. There are spirits that enjoy the pain and suffering of their victims, so manipulating sensations in areas can cause pain throughout the body.

Fever

Just like the way the body reacts to an invading virus or bacteria, the body can react to an invading energy like a spirit. Since the body doesn't understand the difference between the two energies, it reacts with the same protective elements it would normally. Fevers that occur regularly without reason can indicate the invasion of a spirit. This is a less common symptom, so this should only be investigated if all other logical explanations have been ruled out.

Rash or Inflammation

Normally symptoms your body expresses when the body is being invaded by a foreign element. Rashes indicate an inflamed area where energy is being disrupted or wounded. If someone were to have a large rash on their body without any physical symptoms or logical explanations, investigating an attachment would be warranted.

Digestive Disorders

Spirits that bury deep into the solar plexus chakra most often will disrupt the normal digestive operations of the body. Any imprints and abnormalities in the stomach or digestive system would be enough to aid in the creation of or worsen heavy digestive pain, upset, bloating, ulcers, indigestion, chronic digestive issues, bleeding, and illnesses.

Headaches

Headaches are another very common symptom for people with attachments. Migraines, pounding headaches, piercing pain in the head around the ears, or constant pressure can indicate spirit attack when other factors are ruled out. Oftentimes this happens when the spirit is trying to merge in with your mind.

Abrasion, Scratches, or Bruises

This is usually from a negative spirit attachment that is trying to scare or harm the person they are invading. Burning on the skin, scratches, abrasions, bleeding, bruises, or any other skin irritations can indicate an attachment or spirit attack. Spirits can manifest energy within and on the body of the host, creating a wound to inflict pain. If anyone experiences wounds without any clear reasoning or logical explanation that occurs more than once, an attachment investigation should be completed.

MENTAL

Hearing Voices

Again, this is when spirits invade the ears and throat chakra. The vast majority of people do not have schizophrenia, so hearing voices should not be a common thing, yet it is for those gifted to hear it. This is because our senses are becoming more sensitive to spirit energy around us. In the past few years, hearing noises or voices has become more common than before. Hearing certain negative voices or threatening voices could indicate a spirit attachment or attack.

Seeing Hallucinations

Once the invading spirit buries deep within the mind, they can do a great deal of damage. Showing you negative images to scare you or making you see things that aren't there to frighten you can happen. In this way it gives the spirit the power to control you. We rely heavily on believing what we see, so focusing their attention towards your sight builds a strong form of control over you.

Nightmares

Nightmares are another powerful form of control through your mind. Giving you nightmares at night will not only make you fatigued and weary from lack of sleep, but it can scare you and hurt you psychologically. Quite often attachments will send you frightening images when you close your eyes, making it hard to go to sleep.

EMOTIONAL and PSYCHOLOGICAL

Anger

A person experiencing severe rage, anger, or frustration all the time should be considered a high risk candidate for an attachment. Anger is one of the most common emotional symptoms since the spirits that look to harm people carry a lot of anger inside. The emotions of the spirit start to merge with the emotions of the host, making them linked together emotionally. Anger can be a symptom of depression and anxiety, so getting a proper diagnosis or doctor's opinion should be completed before considering the possibility of an attachment. Individuals who experience severe anger rarely want to be seen by a doctor, so healing modalities or calming techniques should be utilized to help minimize the experienced frustration.

Intense Highs and Lows

People who suddenly exhibit signs of bipolar disorders or severe anxiety could indicate a possible attachment. The fluctuation of mixed emotions could indicate several entities or spirits within a person. Professional medical examination should be completed first before considering treatment for an attachment. Barring physical or mental issues, an attachment is a more common diagnosis for those who have never experienced any kinds of psychological issues before but suddenly take on extreme changes to their personality.

Depression

Onset of severe depression should raise the question of whether someone has a spirit attachment. Feelings of sadness, loneliness, or becoming indifferent to everything normally indicate someone with depression. Depression can be hard to diagnose and should always be followed up with a specialized doctor. Depression can lead to far worse situations, so getting the necessary help should be obtained. Investigation of an attachment should be in conjunction with specialized and professional help.

Anxiety

Feelings of paranoia, extreme anxiousness, or fear can be a symptom of an attachment. The invading spirit signals to the body that something is wrong, giving off warning signs like feelings of being watched, of being attacked, or of being confined or held hostage. All symptoms are indications that something is wrong within the mind and body of the host. Often these feelings indicate a psychological imbalance or disorder, so getting professional counseling should be done first. If symptoms do not improve through treatment, attachment investigation is suggested.

Sexual Changes

A person with an attachment can start acting out and demanding sexual intercourse or sexual activities more often. Earthbound spirits that attach to people to harass them sexually will also merge with the mind to make the victim or host want sexual stimulation frequently. In this way, the spirit can have sexual relations with other people through the use of the host's body.

Clearing Team

There really are countless reasons why spirits attach to people, so you're going to need to take it one attachment at a time to learn how to handle the situation. There aren't any one-size-fits-all directions to this work, so use trial and error to find what works best for you. Remember that what works for one situation won't always work for another. This is when learning multiple ways to remove attachments will be beneficial to your training and work. Removal of attachments can be difficult because not only will you need to protect yourself, others in the room, and the host of the attachment, but you're also going to need to protect the attachment as well. Trying to remove attachments by yourself can be risky, so always try to have at least one other medium, healer, clearer, or attachment removal specialist with you. Alongside other working clearers, you're going to need to call in certain spiritual guides and mentors. This is what I call your clearing team. Each member will work differently depending on their own unique style and culture, but the team should normally consist of:

Protectors

Ascended masters, archangels, saints, or any other spiritual warrior that can assist with protection.

Animal Protectors

Your personal animal protectors in spirit should always be standing by to protect you and your energy. Animal protectors usually present themselves beside you, shielding you from attack.

Healers

Archangels, saints, angels, mentors like doctors or nurses, guides, and animal spirits. Elementals may also come in to help maintain the balance of energy within a space and the surrounding Earth elements.

Shepherding Spirits

There are teams on the other side that specialize in helping spirits transition. They usually fall under the guidance of archangels and ascended masters. Usually they carry a heavier vibration, but lighten their energy once the spirit is ready to move on. Quite often these shepherding spirits will lead the spirit into the light with their guides and angels.

Spirit Police

Spiritual protectors that oversee spiritual law may step in when they feel the free will of the host or spirit is being compromised. They will usually remove the spirit from the host once all ties of acceptance are removed.

Guides

Guides that serve the host, the spirit, and all mediums in the room will come in for extra support. Always look to your guides for help and reassurance that your clearing work is done correctly. They will influence your judgement and decision making when completing a spirit attachment removal.

Removing the Attachment

The most common type of attachment you're going to be working on are those of negative spirits. So I'm going to concentrate more on explaining the removal of negative spirits through physical, mental, energetic, and spiritual techniques. The techniques that follow can be used for all forms of spirit attachments; however, the more forceful techniques should be used only in occurrences of negative or harassing spirits.

As a medium, you might be approached by someone who believes they have an attachment. Usually this is through the computer, phone, or in person. You should always shield yourself and call in members of your clearing team even if you do not have the person in front of you. Just the act of thinking of them or talking to them on the phone creates enough of a link to allow the spirit attachment to merge with your energy and attach to you. This is done through energy cords. When you think of that person, you send a signal of energy to them, alerting the attachment to who you are. So don't think you're safe from attack just because the person isn't physically with you. Protection must start from the beginning, even before you start the attachment removal. Mediums that pick up attachments from others usually do this when they first meet the client or when the subject is introduced to them through someone who knows the client. Energy cords can run through people, including from the client directly to you, so always be on guard.

Setting up a time and place for the attachment removal must be handled carefully, just like setting up an indirect rescue circle. Pick your time, place, and co-workers wisely. Do not try to help others when you are sick or tired yourself, as you will need to be at your best in order to fully protect yourself and everyone else. Try to make sure the only guests at the attachment removal area are qualified to handle the situation. I strongly discourage removal around any children, around the home or place of business, as well as near anyone elderly or sick. If the person cannot protect themselves confidently, then they shouldn't be around to watch. Even having someone else in the house or office during the time of the removal can be at risk, so try to have the place cleared of all other guests first. If you plan on having this done in the person's home, try to find a time that meets their needs. Quiet and peaceful times during the day work best.

Setting up the right intention in the space will be important. You want to try to control and stimulate the energy in the room before you allow your host to come in. I like to set up candles for intent, incense to help stimulate the energy, and crystals to raise the vibration of the room. Clearing and healing crystals are best at this time. I try to stay away from any crystals with a heavy vibration. The point is to raise the vibration of the room and the vibration of the host.

The best advice I can give you for all attachment removal is to change the frequency of the vibration. A great many spirits that attach to a person carry a lower vibration than the host. The lower vibration within the host is an indicator that the person has an attachment, along with other symptoms the person is having. In order to push out or eliminate the attachment, you must make the host an uncomfortable environment for the attachment. This means raising the vibrational frequency within the person with the attachment to make it uncomfortable enough to detach and release from the host. This can take multiple attempts depending on how deep the attachment is in the person and how capable the host is to letting go.

One would assume that people who have the attachment would want them to be released right away. Usually this is true, but there are a few reasons why the person with the attachment might struggle with the release of the spirit, making it difficult to remove. Reasons would include:

Fear

The host of the attachment has been mentally and emotionally compromised enough to fear the attachment and doesn't wish to anger it any more. The attachment could become aggressive toward the host, lashing out at them every time the host thinks about removing them. Thoughts and images of frightening subjects may be shown to the host as well, or the attachment may threaten to kill the host if they even try to remove them.

Giving Up

The host of the attachment can be so weary of their situation, that they wish to just give up and give in to the attachment. People may go a very long time with the attachment, draining them of all peaceful or happy memories they had before the attachment. Giving in to the attachment stops the daily struggle, allowing the host to rest.

They Don't Believe

Trust is a big issue for those with attachments. The spirit has dashed all hopes that the host will be free of their torment. Attachments also feed the host lies, allowing them to believe that they can't trust anyone. It may be that the host has tried many times to remove the spirit through the use of mediums and clearers without luck. The breaking down of hope in the mind of the host can create a situation that makes it hard for the host to let go of the attachment.

Lack of Control

Any fear associated with lack of trust, faith, and control over the situation is enough to draw the attachment back into the host. You may try several attempts to remove the attachment, but if the host doesn't have the will to keep them out, there's nothing you can do to block the spirit from attaching again. The host is essentially enabling the situation. The free will of the host needs to be completely compromised in order for spiritual protectors to step in. If the host fears the spirit will return, then they don't believe they have control. If they don't believe they have control, then essentially, they are allowing the spirit to have control. Consequently, this signals to the spirit that they are allowed to come back in. Only when the host can protect themselves without the help from others, can they be completely free from the attachment. This level of personal control must be affirmed at all times.

Comfort of the Familiar

Even when something is painful, the host can sometimes crave the comfort of the familiar and not let go of the attachment. In life there are people who do not like change, no matter how beneficial it will be to them. They will hold onto the attachment until they are too drained of energy due to physical or mental illness.

Building a Bond

Hosts that have a hard time letting go of the spirit because they've built a dependency on them. Spirits try to attach on to people with low self-esteem for this very reason. Attachments can temporarily build up a person's ego, making them feel strong, just so the host won't look for help and release them. Oftentimes this occurs when spirits are trying to hide in the hosts for an extended period of time. If the host doesn't mind them being there, then there's no reason to go.

Once the decision has been made by both the clearer and the host to remove the spirit attachment, the removal can begin. To start, I usually have the client sit comfortably in a chair or couch so that they feel at ease. I may need them to lie down on a massage or healing table if the attachment needs more forceful removal. I begin by communicating with the spirit through mental thought transfer or telepathy. By communicating with the spirit I can try to influence them to release from the host and move on. Direct rescue techniques are used to try to help the spirit release any negative imprints, though that usually will not work. In general, negative spirits do not wish to be helped and will only find your counseling humorous or frustrating. At this time, I give the spirit ample opportunities to move on before I get aggressive with their removal. Then the spirit will most likely fight back energetically or ignore me completely.

Removing a negative attachment can be handled in various ways, and I recommend using several techniques at the same time since they support each other. Techniques to help remove earthbound spirits are: physical tools, emotional conditioning of the host, energetic stimulation, and spiritual help.

Physical Tools

Singing Bowls

These are a great tool to use to help raise the vibration in the room and around the host. I'll usually move the singing bowls around each chakra, stimulating a high-pitched octave around the attachment, making them uncomfortable in the high vibrational environment. Though this doesn't remove the attachment completely, it helps to loosen their grip a little.

High Vibrational Crystals

You can use whichever crystals that you like as long as they carry a very high vibration. I place them on the areas of the host where I believe the attachment may be buried into. Just like the singing bowls, they change the internal frequency of the host, making the spirit uncomfortable.

Smudging

Not only useful in clearing, this technique doesn't directly clear attachments, but it does strip away energetic layers of negativity that allows for healing energy to move in. If the outer shell of energy is dense and thick, then removal of the entity can be hard and time consuming. So stripping layers of energetic baggage is helpful.

Religious Relics

If you are a firm believer in using spiritual or religious relics like crosses, holy water, or the Bible, then please feel free to use them. These items will help bring in more positive energy into the room and reaffirm the support of higher spiritual protectors.

Emotional Conditioning of the Host

This should be something that occurs in the beginning, during, and after the clearing. Making sure the host removes any and all connections to the attachment are important. Working on building up the host's confidence through prayers, affirmations, and exercises to increase their free will, will allow the host to gain control over the situation. There are times when professional counseling is needed along with attachment removal, especially if the host has mental and emotional imprints from life that the spirit has anchored into. This includes personal negative imprints from childhood trauma, abusive relationships, or negative environments. All will be used against them during the time of the attachment. Spirits can anchor into these imprints, making the host mentally relive the emotional trauma. Most importantly, the mental and emotional imprints need to be removed through supportive counseling so that the spirit has nothing left to hold onto.

Energetic Stimulation

Hands-on healing or any form of healing like Reiki that raises the vibration of the host is concentrated on during this time. This is when you move into the host's energy and help push out negative imprints that the spirit has attached to. I'll usually move behind the client and perform an energetic cleanse and clearing of all chakras. This helps to not only push out negative imprints from the chakras, but also stimulate the chakras, creating a strong and vibrant energy flow through the host's body. Remember to set up a shield of protection that only allows energy to flow into the host and not back up into you. Visualizing special bracelets around my hands with protective energy usually works for me. The steps I take to cleanse the chakras are:

· Move through each chakra starting at the crown, working down to the root. Place your hand around each area that is associated with a chakra.
· Visualize yourself pushing white light from your hands into the chakra until all energy that feels dense, heavy, or dark is gone. If you feel resistance, push gold energy into it until the resistance is gone.
· Once all chakras are cleared of imprints, go back and visualize pushing the color associated with each chakra into them. For example, push violet into the crown, push indigo into the third eye, push light blue into the throat, and so on.
· Finish the chakra cleanse by imagining a golden stream of energy flowing down through the body of the host starting at the tip of their head, working

down through their feet. This is what I call the golden flush. The golden energy pushes all heavy and dense energy out of the body by filling up the body with the highest protective color associated with the Christ energy. Keep pushing golden energy through the body until all resistance is eliminated.

- Have your clearing team remove all remaining residual energy that was pushed out of the feet. They will take and transmute this energy for the best intent of the universe.

Spiritual Help

This is probably one of the most important steps of your attachment removal. Since you are working with spiritual energy, it's best to use your spiritual team and clearers to help remove the attachment from the host. All steps that came before this were ways to remove the grip the attachment had on the host and prepare for the actual removal of the attachment by your spiritual team.

I usually start by asking my angelic protectors and warriors to reaffirm the removal request to the spirit, making the earthbound spirit aware that they have broken spiritual law by inhibiting the free will of the host. Spirit police and angelic protectors will usually start by pulling out the spirit from the host. Once I see the protectors doing this, I simultaneously cut any cords connecting the spirit attachment to the host. You can cut energetic cords through visualization or just by feeling the energy cord between the host and the spirit. If you do not see or feel the energy cords, just imagine cords connecting the host and the spirit and cut them to disconnect the energetic connection. I'll sometimes use a visualization of golden scissors or a golden knife to cut these energetic cords. Once the cords have been severed, I send white light into the gap of the host where the attachment was housed.

Spiritual clearers will usually take over and give instructions to the spirit on what happens next. If the spirit does not follow them into the light to finish their transition, then these clearers will take them to a holding area for a limited time. Spiritual healers will try to influence the spirit by sending them healing and love. If the energetic healing is accepted by the spirit, they are likely to be willing to transition into the light.

There are times when the spirit breaks free from the clearers and moves down into a lower vibration, escaping to a different level of existence. The clearers usually won't follow them into that realm. As long as the attachment has been removed and the host relieved of their abuser, the clearers will usually let things go for the moment. I'll usually watch and observe the spiritual exchange between the earthbound spirit and the clearing team. This allows me to understand what is happening and know how much protection I need to give the client. Since I'm not working alone, I'll have another clearer or healer work with the client by continuing hands-on healing or energetic healing to help remove all residual energy from the attachment.

Once the attachment has been removed by the spiritual clearing team, I thank them for their help and offer my love and support to them. My team and I work very well together. You need to know that you cannot do any of this work without your spiritual team. It's a team effort, and you need to realize that from the start.

When all spiritual clearers have left and the host feels at ease with the removal, I'll work by removing all residual energy from the room through residual energy removal techniques. Remind the client to continue working on self-esteem building exercises so that the host won't draw in the attachment again. Always remember to clear yourself of all residual energy as well as any other mediums or clearers in the room.

CHAPTER FIFTEEN
Nonhuman Entities

While working in the field of spirit rescue, you may come across several different energy forms other than earthbound spirits. I know we work with our spiritual team on the other side to assist in our work, but the energy sources I'm referring to would be lower entities or manifested energy clusters that mimic demonic entities. I usually try to persuade rescuers to stay away from lower-level entities as they are not in need of rescue or counseling, but you will need to know what these entities are and how to handle them as they appear throughout your work. There will be times when demonic entities or energy projections attach onto an earthbound spirit, influencing them not to cross. So learning how to handle these entities and clearing them away will be helpful in your rescue work.

Most people in the physical world cannot tell the difference between a lower-level entity and a really dark and negative earthbound spirit. That's because the vibration can sometimes be the same. Dark earthbound spirits may try to persuade people that they are demons to provoke fear and anxiety. They do this to gain control through fear. It's only natural for us here to be concerned when faced with dark energy and to assume that these are demons. Earthbound spirits that move into a very low vibration can seem very demonic. Their essence of who they were when connected to Divine energy has faded away, leaving only a dark shell of energy in its place. Just like when we ascend to higher realms connecting back in with the Divine energy, we can also move so far away from it that we disconnect ourselves indefinitely. The earthbound spirit has to move down into such a lower state of consciousness in order for this to happen, but it can and does happen. The earthbound spirit, when in such a low state, can will itself to no longer exist. Its energy dissipates and the intelligence within the spirit mind fades. This is the state of consciousness that many people refer to as Hell. As I always say, Heaven and Hell are not places, they are vibrations within a consciousness that either connects you back to Divine energy or removes you from it. But just like in Heaven where many different forms of entities and angelic beings exist, Hell also houses many energy forms within its different vibrational levels as well. As you descend down into the lower realms, you connect with different life forms.

In my experience working in rescue work, I've had to come in contact with several different entities, both good and bad, and wanted to share my thoughts on what I believe these entities are and how to tell the difference between them. I'm not going into detail about demonic entities in very low levels of consciousness as we rarely deal with them in our rescue work. I want to concentrate on the forms of entities you will come across so that you are better prepared. The five main categories of lower-level entities that I've experienced are:

1. Demonic entities
2. Lower-realm angels
3. Lower-level elementals
4. Energy clusters
5. Projections

Demonic Entities

Truly understanding demonic entities can be very difficult as many of us would rather keep our distance from them rather than learn more about them. In my experiences of demonic entities, I've come across three different forms. The first would be considered the scouts. They are small and less dangerous as they roam around seeking out people who have very low self-esteem, who are sick, who are unable to defend themselves or those who provoke lower entities with games or rituals.

They cannot do any real harm, but can surround a person's energy, to lower it enough for a stronger demonic entity to attach to. Think of them as the insects of the lower realm. There are countless numbers of these in the physical world. The best way to protect yourself from these entities is to stay above the radar. This means to keep your vibration at a high enough level so that they do not feel comfortable around you. Detecting these scouts can be difficult because they carry a slightly higher vibration than heavy demonic entities. Their personalities are devious and they will seem more like tricksters than evil beings.

The second form of demonic entity would be what I consider the soldiers or army. They do most of the damage out in the physical world. Many of these demonic entities have names, which they give their victims so that the victims understand who they are dealing with. They want to be known. Each entity has one main purpose, and that is to strip away all good from a person and to separate them from the Divine source. They seem to believe that if they lower a person's vibration, they can increase the lower-level consciousness, making their realm larger and stronger. Just like many different energy forms, their focus is to take control and dominate. They do this through control of our energy. I've personally seen a few of these entities. They've presented themselves to me as a black angel with red eyes. Though I felt their strength and intelligence within them, I knew they didn't have any real control over me unless I gave over my free will to them.

The third form of demonic entity would be what I consider the council. These are very low and dark entities that oversee all demonic activity within the physical and non-physical realms. They very rarely leave the low-level consciousness as they cannot maintain their vibration in our higher realm of the physical world. That's why they send out the scouts and their army to do the work. I haven't seen any manifested form of these entities as they only appear as very dark and dense energy forms.

So why are these entities even allowed to exist since they are so far removed from the Divine energy? I believe it has something to do with the balance of all energy and the manifestations of free will. Free will allows us the right to turn away from the Divine source. It's allowed because it's a way of learning more about ourselves and our connection to God. How are we to truly understand our connection to God if we aren't able to experience the absence of it? This is through our free will. Just like human entities, other life forms are able to move away from the Divine source and experience the absence of love and light to learn from it. It's always in the hope of Divine will that these entities will eventually find their way back into the light and the loving embrace of God. This is why the lower realms are overseen by angels that, when allowed, redirect these entities back to God when the entity is ready.

Lower-Realm Angels

Just like angels that oversee activities within the higher realms of Heaven, these angelic forces oversee activity in the lower realm. These angels try to maintain a certain level of control over the energy being maintained in the lower levels. They also provide assistance to the entities within that realm. I believe angels who were put down into the lowest of realms to oversee demonic entities as being some of the brightest and most loving of angels. Their true unconditional love and support to these entities cannot be broken even when the entities are at their worst. The angels provide the option to return back into the light when the free will of the demonic entity changes. Even the council members of the lower realms cannot interfere with the free will of the demons or the support the angelic energies have over them. This is seen as the force of God within all realms that cannot be overturned. Even the council members know their place.

The battle over Heaven and Hell isn't what people have been taught to believe. It's more controlled and balanced than that. If you begin to understand the reasons behind the darkness and fear, you start to grasp the bigger picture of it all. It's all about learning, developing, and evolving as entities created by God or the creator source. Sometimes you need to lose something in order to understand how important it was. This is why the absence of God was created.

Lower-Level Elementals

As our consciousness is evolving and expanding to explore more realms and entities in the Universe, we encounter many entities that may seem negative in nature but are actually very protective. Gnomes, undines, sylphs, and salamanders are classified as elementals. They are very old and powerful entities that regulate elements pertaining to Earth, air, fire, and water. Know that when you aggravate an elemental, they can seem very dangerous and evil in nature. That's only because of the strong force of dense energy they present themselves with. They are trying to protect the Earth, and when they feel something is being threatened, they can attack.

It's best to stay on the good side of elementals. I once had an elemental attachment for several months. It seemed very demonic in nature as it moved around my body and across my face. It wanted me to know it had full control and really wanted to get my attention. When I connected in with the entity, it demanded that it was from the light and only wanted to get a message through to me. I asked what the message was, and it said it was something I was going to be told at the right time. I carried this entity with me for months as it drained me of all my energy. When it came time for me to do some clearing work, it became very forceful and put a lot of pressure around my head. It showed me that what I was doing wrong. Throughout my training, I was always told to transmute negative energy by pushing it down into Mother Earth's energy and allowing the Earth to absorb it. I had been doing that for years. This elemental was very unhappy that I was doing that. I said that the Earth was already under a lot of stress and had taken in many wounds from humans; it didn't need our negative energy getting pushed into it as well. We were damaging Earth's energy by sending it our energetic trash. I felt so bad because I was always told that the Earth could transmute it and change it to something beneficial. The elemental informed me that in the past it was allowed, but the Earth is under so much stress right now it can't handle the extra negative energy. That's when I started asking my angelic clearers to take the energy away and use it for good use in the Universe. That seemed to work much better. The elemental was content with my change and left my body. It wanted to stay attached to me for some time to allow me to understand how strong and powerful the entity was. I now respect and honor elementals in their work.

Energy Clusters

Energy clusters manifest similarly to residual energy clusters—though this energy doesn't manifest only from past situations; they can also include situations that are occurring at the present time. If you condense enough energy together, it can manifest into its own intelligence. Think of energy like sand and negative thoughts and emotions like water. Combine the two and it turns into mud. You can condense enough mud together that it forms into a structure that seems very similar to a demonic entity. The difference is the demonic entity originated from a lower realm, while the dense energy cluster was created by the ones feeding the energy. For example, if a very abusive father lived in a home with two children whom he hurt emotionally and physically, he would manifest a very dense and heavy energetic cluster in the house. Every time he abused the children, he would add to this cluster of energy, condensing it and making it stronger. So it may seem very evil in nature, when in fact it's just condensed energy. But just like any energy in the Universe, it can evolve and change over time. These energy clusters will most often feel very evil, but usually won't manifest into a semi-physical apparition or image. It's more like walking into a house and feeling something evil watching you. That's because the energy is looking to grow stronger, so it looks for other energy sources to feed off of. It can and will attach onto you like a demonic attachment but will usually withdraw from you if you quickly raise your vibration.

Projections

Projections work a little differently than clusters of energy because, unlike energy clusters that manifest out in the open, projections manifest from within you. Everyone experiences bad or negative situations from time to time. Most have enough coping skills to deal with the situation while others do not. There are times when people experience so much negativity in their life that they learn to shield themselves from the situation by trying to forget about it. They think they are helping themselves by ignoring the situation or trying to keep their mind off of it, but the negative feelings and thoughts create their own imprint, and that imprint has to go somewhere if you don't release it. That's when this imprint gets submerged into the subconscious and into the chakras. This happens on occasion, yet many people do not realize they are doing it. Over time, the subconscious and chakras that take on these imprints start to get overwhelmed and overstimulated. While trying to protect itself, the body's energy projects the energy imprint out to you to get you to pay attention to it. If you address the imprint and release it, then the body's energy can heal.

Nightmares, hallucinations, panic attacks, physical pain, depression, and headaches can all be signs of projections that your body is alerting you to. Over time, these imprints that get submerged into your chakras can manifest into a dense and negative energy. This negative energy within your body may seem like a demonic attachment when in fact it's your own subconscious thoughts and emotions that manifested. Once the submerged emotions and negative thought imprints are healed and released, the manifested energy dissipates. You can usually tell when someone has a projection instead of a demonic entity because all signs lead back to trauma the person experienced.

There are countless other entities in the Universe that are both positive and negative, which we are just beginning to connect to and understand. As you work on clearing attachments and imprints from your clients, you may come across many energy life beings that are just attempting to learn from us or use us as a host. Not all are going to be damaging to us, so choose your battles wisely. Over time we shall learn enough to not only protect ourselves from entities from other realms but to also obtain knowledge and experience through them.

CHAPTER SIXTEEN
Clearing Yourself

We've covered a lot of information in this book that I hope really helps you along with your journey into rescue work. There is one topic I'd like to mention that happens to be the most important part of your work. This is something that, if missed, will threaten you and your work because of the damage it will do to you. This is the topic of clearing yourself. I can't begin to explain how extremely important this is for you. The amount of energy that you will be working with can stick to you like a sponge and suck your energy dry, not to mention the amount of attachments and energy imprints you'll pick up. You have to make sure you learn how to clear yourself well so that your safety and welfare will never be compromised.

You're not going to need to clear yourself the same way after each situation. There are quite a few different ways to clear yourself, from doing a quick clearing to a whole day clearing and cleanse of your energy. The work you've been doing will determine what type of clearing you're going to need to do. The longer you go between clearings, the longer it will take to completely cleanse yourself of dense and heavy energy. And remember, we aren't just looking to clear ourselves of negative energy we've picked up, we are going to want to cleanse ourselves from energy exchanges we encounter daily.

Whenever I do clearing work on myself, I usually commit to repeating a certain form of clearing work on myself three times. The number three represents a cycle. The first time to open the intent, the second time to affirm the intent, and the third time to close the intent. This can either be done three times a day for a daily cleanse, three consecutive days of clearing for a slightly larger cleanse, three consecutive weeks of clearing for a large and intense cleanse, or a three-month cleanse for a complete shift of energy. If you should feel that the cleanse or clearing wasn't effective enough and you're still experiencing symptoms, repeat the cycle again and see how you feel.

So, how can you tell if you need to cleanse your energy? There are different ways to determine this depending on how sensitive you are to changes of energy on and around your body. The three main ways to sense and feel if you need an energy clearing is through physical, non-physical, and psychological.

Physical

Physical symptoms that alert you to a need for a clearing and cleansing of your energy will be fatigue, mental fog, joint pain, stomach bloating, headaches, tightness around the neck and shoulders, muscle cramping, ringing in the ears, throat tightness, chest pain or palpitations, bowel changes, or pain, sickness, and illnesses.

Non-Physical

Non-physical symptoms should probably alert you first to an energy cleanse since you're a sensitive and intuitive person. Working around energy will give you a great deal of experience on reading energy. Symptoms may include heavy feelings in certain parts of your aura, blockages in your chakras, feeling blocked from opening up psychically, mental images or nightmares, sensing another life energy connected to you, feelings of heavy pressure around your head, or flashes of dark energy around you.

Psychological

Symptoms that effect you psychologically are feelings of sadness, anger, frustration, lack of will power, low self-esteem, anxiety, racing thoughts, fear, loneliness, or other feelings that are negative in nature. Taking on emotions and feelings right after a rescue that mimic the spirit's emotions can alert you to a residual imprint you've received from the spirit.

You're not going to experience all of these symptoms right after your rescue work, as some of these symptoms take time to manifest. Energy changes are much faster than physical matter changes. This means your body is going to need time to catch up to the shift or change in energy. It could take a day or two for the symptoms to start manifesting. That's why I always recommend clearing yourself right after you work. This minimizes the chances for the energy to gain strength and attach deeper into your aura.

There are five different clearing and cleansing techniques I use to help me clear myself after each rescue, attachment removal, residual energy clearing, psychic work, or mediumship reading. These techniques are:

1. Visualization
2. Energy clearing with tools

3. Cleansing with Earth elements
4. Raising vibration through meditation
5. Receiving healing and cleansing energy from my spiritual team

Visualization

Like any other energy work you've done before, visualization for clearing your own energy will be performed the same way. By seeing the energy in your mind, you can change and remove it through thought and intent. I will start off by sensing the energy on or in my body due to the change in frequency in a particular spot. It will usually feel heavier or more intense in that area, so sensing it will be easy. Try to pay close attention to how your body feels before and after you work. If you get a strong and heavy feeling in your gut after you do a clearing on another person, this may indicate you've picked up the energy you removed from your client. I know we work hard on shielding ourselves when we work, but mistakes are made, and energy may sometimes find a way to get through. Try not to be hard on yourself if this happens.

Once I've detected the area on my body that needs to be cleared, I'll start imagining the dense and heavy energy changing to manifest into a cluster of energy on or in me. This helps condense it so that it's easier to move around. Once it's easier to move around, I can work on my visualization of pushing the cluster out of my body and energy. Earlier we used a visualization to help form a shield around us, we can use this visualization to help push out any dense clusters of energy from within or on us as well.

Start with your core, which is the space just under your heart chakra that you visualize like a bright ball of white energy. It is actually your lower heart chakra that doesn't get used as much as your higher heart chakra. (Yes, you have two). The lower heart chakra connects you to your higher self. This is why I call it the core of who you are. Allow this bright, white energy to shine within your chest and radiate within your body. Start imagining the white light expanding through your body, pushing out any heavy or dense energy, including your heavy energy cluster. Allow the white light from your core to detach this energy cluster and push it out or off your body. Form another shield of energy around you with the white light and encase it within a protection color of your choice. If you should feel resistance of the energy cluster, surround the energy cluster with golden light to help raise its vibration. Once the vibration is higher, it can be more easily moved. You may notice dark energy imprints removing themselves from your body when you push white light out from your core. This is great and is supposed to happen.

If you should feel energy clusters or imprints within your chakras while you are doing this visualization, start to penetrate the white light from your core into your chakras. This will flush out any residual imprints that do not originate from you. This can be any energy that you've picked up over time from other people, places, and events that have anchored into your chakra. Penetrate the chakra with white light and raise the internal vibration so that all heavy residual imprints are pushed out along with all other residual imprints from your body.

Once you've pushed out all residual or spirit imprints from within your body, you will finish your visualization with a golden flush. In the same way that we flushed out all remaining residual energy with golden light during an attachment session, we would do the same on ourselves. Start at the top of your head and push gold light down through your body allowing all residual energy to move down and out of you. Ask your guides, angels, or energy healers to take the energy coming out of your feet and use it for good somewhere else in the universe. All energy can be beneficial one way or another. Just because it's not good for us, doesn't mean it can't be used to make a star or help a volcano erupt. Energy isn't inherently good or evil. It just is. How you use it determines its advantage.

This energy visualization not only works for residual energy, but it can also work to help clear attachments. By creating a very high vibrational frequency in your body, you create an uncomfortable environment for your negative attachment. If you should have an attachment that isn't negative, then the attachment will gain some healing and comfort from this energy shift. Everyone benefits from raising your vibration. Perform this visualization again and again until the spirit attachment releases. Over time, the high energy will break their hold on you, releasing them from your body.

Energy Clearing with Tools

Using tools in your clearing work will help maintain a high vibration around you when you work on your visualization. Stripping layers of residual energy around you and breaking up energy clusters in your home helps maximize the success of your clearing work within you. A few tools that I use to help clear my energy are:

Personal Smudging

I'll smudge myself before and after my work just to make sure I'm not transferring residual energy to my client, and I'm not transferring residual energy from them. If I should feel that I still absorbed energy imprints from them, then I'll smudge myself two more times to complete the energy cycle. Burn incense or herbs in a fire resistant object to create smoke to smudge with. Fan this smoke all around you and your space. Doing this helps remove residual layers of energy off your aura. It also makes it easier to help push imprints out of you. The fewer layers you have, the less friction you'll receive in your cleanse. Smudging doesn't help raise your vibration, as it's meant to help neutralize energy and to set thought and intent.

Absorbing Crystals

I'll use cleansing crystals to help remove any residual imprints from my body. I'll place crystals on my chakra points, which correlate with each chakra, to help cleanse and recharge them. Or, I'll place a smoky quartz crystal on my abdomen to help eliminate residual energy from my aura. Smoky quartz is a great absorbing crystal. I find it's one of the best to use for residual imprints.

Salt

As I've mentioned, salt is great for neutralizing your energy during or after your visualization. Often people like to place their feet in a salt bath to neutralize the energy coming out of their feet instead of giving it over to their clearing guides. This works as well. Remember that the energy will get absorbed into the salt, so rinse the salt down the drain or flush it away. Another way to use salt is by washing yourself in the bath or shower with a salt/soap mixture. This helps cleanse your body energetically and physically.

Sound

Chimes, singing bowls, or bells work well to break up energy clusters on or around your body. It helps to raise the vibration, much like crystals. You can buy singing bowls that carry the tone for each chakra and play them above each chakra. I'll do the same by singing the notes or playing the notes that correlate to each chakra to push out energy clusters. I recommend singing them so that the frequency of the note comes from within your body. This helps regenerate the chakra and stimulate its energy. Start at the root and work up to the crown chakra. To help understand which tone to use for each chakra, I use DO, RE, MI to help.

Do: Root
Re: Sacral
Mi: Solar plexus
Fa: Heart
So: Throat
La: Third eye
Ti: Crown
And I'll end with Do: Soul (star chakra)
—white in color, just above the crown chakra.

Clearing with Earth or Universal Elements

The Earth's energy can be so healing and cleansing. Many people around the world use energy from the Earth to help restore, replenish, and energize their chi, auras, and chakras. I certainly recommend connecting in with Earth's elements to reap the benefits of these healing powers. Try to remember that even though the Earth is strong and vibrant, it can be harmed and wounded, just like us. Every time you ask for healing energy from these elements, try to replenish the energy taken from the Earth with something you can give back. Plant a tree, recycle, use less toxifying chemicals, clean up trash, or anything else that gives back to mother nature. I like to send healing energy back into the Earth through meditation and visualization. Every time I connect my root chakra into the Earth, I imagine sending healing energy down through this link, deep into a root in the Earth. I'll imagine this energy spreading out into the ground, sending it to various sources that are in need of healing. Do what works for you, but try to remember that healing is something that should be given as well as received. Elements that I use that help cleanse my energy are:

Earth

Stones: I use stones from all over the world to help cleanse my energy. By placing these stones on certain parts of my body or by holding them in my hands, I radiate Mother Earth's energy into my body, healing and energizing it. Stones are a great way to ground yourself quickly to take in deep and heavy energy healing from the Earth.

Dirt: I try to use dirt as a conduit of energy. By visualizing the energy clusters moving out of my body, down through my arms and hands out into the ground, I clear myself of any residual imprint. Think of it like planting residual energy like a flower. Cover the ground and ask the Earth to manifest the energy so that it will be beneficial for growth and renewal.

Trees: Hug a tree, and you'll receive some amazing Earth energy. The roots of the tree act like your root chakra, sending up healing energy. The energy flow moves into you once you physically connect in with the tree. Imagine the energy from the tree filling your body with green healing energy. This will start to energize your chakras, making it easier to raise your vibration.

Air

Breathe: This can be an amazing tool to use to help stabilize your energy. Take a few deep breaths to center yourself and ground yourself for healing. Try using a humidifier with salt crystals to neutralize the air you breathe in. This helps clear energy clusters from your body.

Wind: Wind near the ocean has a wonderful cleansing effect. The salt water from the ocean air is extremely cleansing. The wind blows evaporated salt water towards you, cleansing your body and aura. Imagine dense and heavy energy being cleared away from you with the wind.

Fire

Fire: I'll usually use the fire to aid in my visualization. By setting a bonfire outside or lighting a fire in the fireplace, I can visualize energy running out my body, through my arms and hands, and out into the fire, transmuting it. I allow the fire to absorb the residual energy from me, manifesting it to a better source for the world and universe.

Smoke: Much like smudging, I can use the smoke from the fire to help neutralize the energy around my body. People may like to breathe in the smoke to help neutralize the inside of their body, but I don't recommend that. There's too much harm that can be done to the lungs by breathing in smoke. So please be sure to use the smoke wisely.

Electricity: Can be thought of as either air or fire, depending on your view. Since electricity or lighting can cause the fire element, I will use it with fire. Electricity is a conduit of energy. You can use electricity to absorb the residual energy from your body, flowing it off to another area. In the past, people have used a plasma globe to absorb energy from their hands. By imagining energy transferring from your hands into the streams of electricity, the energy gets trapped into the globe.

Water

Water: By simply taking a shower, bath, or swimming in water you can imagine residual energy being rinsed off you. Using a salt/soap mixture during a shower or bath, you help to neutralize the energy before it goes down the drain. Water is one of the most common cleansing techniques used to help clear residual energy.

Flowing water: Flowing water like rivers, lakes, or streams can be very cleansing as the water can rinse energy off of your body, sending it away from you. Think of it like washing yourself off with the water of Mother Nature. Oceans are wonderful as they allow the cleansing salt to help neutralize residual imprints from your aura.

Sun

The sun is amazing and should be used to cleanse at every chance. After taking a shower or swimming in a flowing body of water, sit under the sun and allow the sunshine to cleanse and clear all remaining residual energy off of you. Not only does it help warm your skin, raise your energy, and make you feel good, the energy from the sun is healing and very beneficial to your overall health. So sit under that sunshine and soak in all the rays. You'll be glad you did.

Raising Vibration through Meditation

Raising your vibration through meditation not only helps you elevate your energy to remove imprints and attachments, but also connects you back in with your guides and angels for mentoring and support. Energy attachments or imprints can hinder us from receiving information from our guides and angels because it lowers our vibration, pushing us away from our higher spiritual healers. If you feel too compromised to sense and receive your guides' help, then raising your vibration will help make your connection and link stronger. I use several meditations to help raise my vibration. This is done through a visualization where I move in an upward motion while energizing my chakras. I'll sometimes imagine walking up white stairs, or climbing a mountain, but for now let me describe the meditation I use.

The Elevator

Sit comfortably in your space, relaxed and calm. Close your eyes and take in three deep breathes to stabilize and ground yourself. From there, we are going to visualize ourselves in a dark room with no windows or doors. Feel warm and safe. This is your starting point for your meditation.

Sense, feel, or imagine yourself in your dark room. Feel secure and safe as nothing can harm you. In front of you, a glowing white and gold elevator presents itself to you. It's shining in the dark room. The sides are made out of mirrors and the edges and sides are encased in gold. I want you to walk over to the elevator and see yourself in the mirror. Pay attention to how you look and feel. Is anyone standing with you or are there any dark spots around your body? On the side of the elevator there are buttons. I want you to push the button that says UP. As you hit this button, the shiny doors open, allowing you to move inside. While inside the elevator, you see the inside of the elevator is the same as the outside. Shining with mirrors and gold. On the inside of the elevator there are more buttons. Hit the button that says TOP FLOOR. This should be all the way at the top of the buttons. As you hit this button, the doors close, and the elevator begins to move upward. You may start to feel your energy shift with this motion. Allow your body to raise its vibration naturally as you ascend upward with the elevator. As you move upward, the lighting in the elevator starts to change.

The brightness turns to a deep red color. Allow this red color to swirl all around you, filling up the inside of the elevator. Once this red color fills the elevator with energy, allow this red color to penetrate into your body, filling you with this red color as well. This is your root. Feel yourself become strong and secure.

As you continue to ascend upward, the red color starts to change to a shining orange color. Allow this bright orange color to swirl all around you and penetrate into your body. This is your sacral. Feel yourself becoming confident and proud. Allow this color to shine from within you until you feel the full effect of this shift.

As you move upward even more, this orange color begins to change to a soft, crisp yellow. Allow this yellow color to swirl all around you and penetrate deep within your body. This is your solar plexus. Feel strong willed and full of joy. Allow yourself to smile and feel happy. Think of it like the sun shining from within you.

As you move upward even more, you start to feel lighter and lighter. This yellow color changes to a deep emerald green. Allow this color to swirl all around you and penetrate deep within you. This is your heart. As you open your heart, you allow this green energy to heal you.

Know that you have the power to heal yourself through the love and support from the divine. As you move upward even more, you start to feel the effects on your body as you become lighter and lighter. The inside of the elevator starts to change as though you are moving out of a deep forest and moving upward into the sky. The color inside the elevator changes to a bright sky blue, as if you are floating in air. Allow this blue to shine all around you and penetrate deep within you. This is your throat and expression. Feel free like a bird and allow yourself to open up and receive love and healing from your guides. Sense and feel yourself expanding out like the wind and connecting in with all elements of the Earth.

As you move even higher, the sky changes as if you are moving out of the atmosphere into space, and an indigo color fills the elevator. Allow this deep bluish-purple color to manifest around you and penetrate deep within you. This is your third eye. Feel the energy of your eye open and connect in with all universal energies. Feel yourself expanding out into space as you become lighter and lighter.

As you move even further up into space, the color inside the elevator changes to a soft violet. This is your crown. This moves you into the spiritual world where your guides and angels are waiting. Allow this violet energy to flow all around you and penetrate deep within you. You are now in a safe place within spirit and divine guidance.

The elevator stops and the doors open. Before you is a white open space. Walk out into the space and greet your guides and angels. They will help you understand what type of healing and clearing work needs to be done. Take time to talk with your guides and angels. When you are ready to leave and come back down, press the button on the elevator that says ground floor. Get back inside the elevator, and feel yourself ground back into your physical body as the elevator descends back downward. This will bring you back into your dark room, where you can allow yourself to slowly come back from your meditation.

Receiving Healing and Cleansing Energy from My Spiritual Team

Not only can we receive useful information from our guides during meditation, but we can also receive healing and clearing energy from them. This can only be done through your request and acceptance. They cannot step in and heal you without your consent. There will be times when your guide and angels take a step back and have you clear yourself on your own. This isn't to harm you, rather to help aid in your training. Knowledge can sometimes only be learned through experience. By having you learn how to clear yourself on your own, guides allow you to gain the knowledge you need for future experiences. The best guides and teachers in the spiritual world will always have you learn how to do things on your own. They would be taking away your strength if they were to do everything for you.

I'll usually ask my guides and healing angels to help clear my energy through prayers. As a Spiritualist, we have a prayer we use to help with healing. Since we are hoping to be healed from all negative attachments, residual imprints, and energy clusters, the prayer we use at the Spiritualist church works well. Please feel free to use whatever prayer you like to call in help from your guides and receive spiritual healing. The prayer for spiritual healing at the Spiritualist church is:

I ask the Great Unseen Healing Force to remove all obstructions from my mind and body and to restore me to perfect health.

I ask this in all sincerity and honesty and I will do my part.

I ask this Great Unseen Healing Force to help both present and absent ones who are in need of help and to restore them to perfect health.

I put my trust in the love and power of God.

Once you recite a prayer for healing, sit comfortably and quietly and allow your guides and angels to channel healing energy into your body. You may feel pressure moving around your body. This is your guides pushing out and removing negative and dense energy from you. Always remember to thank your healing team. They do this with love, so always try to send your love back to them.

Always remember that you are in control. Any compromise that spirit attachments or residual energy gives you is only temporary. Strengthen your confidence and self-assurance to help maintain a strong emotional and mental foundation. Nothing can harm you if you don't allow it. If you should feel that you have been affected in a way that hinders you from clearing yourself, always seek out assistance from those in the psychic and spiritual communities.

CHAPTER SEVENTEEN
Shutting Down

As we all know, living in the physical world is a challenge for some mediums. We get accustomed to connecting with the spiritual world and, for some, get lost in the mystical nature of it all. But we have to remember that we do live in the physical world, and we have physical responsibilities such as a "day job," paying bills, taking care of children or parents, cleaning the house, working on the car, etc. These duties usually do not have any connection to the spirit world, so it's best to shut down our mediumship skills so that we can ground ourselves in our everyday lives. This doesn't mean that we won't have the ability to connect to spirits when we wish, it simply means we're not open to receive all spirit energy around us. We need to focus our attention onto the physical world so that our energy doesn't get drained.

In addition to the aid of grounding for concentration on responsibilities, by shutting down we help protect our energy from lower spirit forms. There are times that the physical world can lower our constant vibration to a state in which all spirits can come through, including lower spirits. Frustration from paying bills, anger while driving, exhaustion from lack of sleep, and so on can and will lower your vibration temporarily, so it's best to keep yourself closed off from spirit during those times.

How to Shut Down

In the same way we learn how to open up our chakras for energy work, we must learn how to close the chakras just enough to refrain from spirit communication. Not all chakras need to be closed. I would recommend keeping your root, sacral, solar plexus, heart, and throat chakras at least half open so that you can maintain a higher vibration on a daily basis. Also, by keeping these half open we can overcome emotional and mental difficulties more easily with a strong energy foundation. The two chakras I would recommend mostly closing are the third eye and crown chakras. Over time, these chakras do get overly stimulated and need to be shut down for rest and recharging. It's best to do that when you aren't prepared to do any psychic or spirit work. Like any muscle in your body, some muscles get used all the time and can handle the more daily wear and tear, while other muscles only get used for specific tasks and need more time to rest. The same is true for your chakras. The third eye and crown chakras work during very specific tasks, so it's best to let them rest after you've used them. You'll find over time that your chakras close automatically on their own when your focus changes to something other than psychic or spirit work and vice versa, your chakras will learn how to automatically open when you start focusing on spirit energy. Your body and energy will let you know when it's ready to work. This can happen at the most inopportune moments, but you'll learn how to control it with more practice.

To close your chakras on your own, visualize your chakra open and glowing full of energy. Sense how strong and focused it is. Now, concentrate on that spot of energy and imagine this shining energy ball start to gradually condense. Bring in all the energy and form it into a small ball. Allow this small ball of energy to release its transfer of energy and relax. Ask for your protective angels and guides to surround your chakras with a shield of protection so that they can't be compromised while you are grounded.

Grounding

After closing all your chakras, you'll need to ground your energy back into your physical body. Yes, your soul is still connected to your physical body, but we are talking about your energy. Your energy expands out and radiates around your body, searching for and reaching out for other energy to read and connect to. By grounding yourself, you are bringing this energy back into your body for shielding and protection. It's similar to a creature or animal that returns to its shell for protection and rest. Your body is your shell that protects your soul and your energy. In bringing your energy back into its shell, you can heal, rest, and recharge for more spirit work later. To begin, we start imagining our energy condensing inside our body. It helps to imagine your energy connecting back in with different parts of your body like chest, abdomen, hips, back, limbs, and feet. Feel the full force of the energy in your body. This may feel very heavy at first, so take your time and go slow. The amount of time it takes to get grounded depends on how high your energy is, how long you've been working with spirit, and the activity in which you try to ground yourself with. As a good estimate, expect about thirty minutes of grounding to feel the full effect, less if you've been grounding yourself for some time and have become good at raising your vibration and lowering it. The more experienced you become, the faster you open and close your energy.

Ways to Help You Ground

Get physical: Do something that makes your body move so that you have to concentrate on your physical self. Go dancing, play a sport or exercise, eat a large meal, or play with the kids. Whatever works for you. Mainly keep yourself active. Before you know it, your mind and body will feel completely grounded, and you'll probably have fun in the process.

Concentrate on daily activities: Keeping your mind focused on daily activities like picking up the kids at school, paying the bills, cooking dinner, walking the dog, going to work, driving, and so on will help you focus back into the "here and now." We can sometimes get lost in time when we connect with spirit, so focusing on when and where we are will help bring our energy down into the physical plane.

Get dirty: Literally. Get yourself dirty with Mother Earth energy by planting flowers, trimming the bushes, raking the yard, collecting rocks or shells, going on a hike in the forest, or digging for worms. Anything that connects you into the Earth's energy will help ground you. The Earth's energy holds a very strong and heavy vibration, but it's a good one. The Earth's energy is dense; however, it's a healing and nurturing force that helps you connect back into your physical self. Not all dense and heavy energy is negative. We need to get over this notion that heavy energy is inherently evil. Heavy energy can be forceful and powerful, which should be honored. Ground yourself into the energy of Mother Earth and take in all the strength and power of this energy to help recharge you. Remember that we are the balance of Earth and spirit. Honor this connection and give back to Mother Earth by helping the planet and sharing your loving energy with her.

Don't Worry About Shutting Down

I have met people who stated that if they completely shut down, they're afraid that they won't be able to open up again. That's a common misconception. It's not like we are closing the door and bolting it with a deadlock. We are closing the door to the spirit world temporarily, leaving it just slightly ajar so that we'll hear if someone comes knocking. The door opens right up again once your energy connects back in with spirit.

For those of you who have closed your door for some time, possibly several years, it takes a little longer to open up like before. Think of it like the door hinges are rusty, and it just needs to be oiled up a bit. Go back and start with foundation work, add a little energy every time you reach a new milestone, and keep working! Remember it may not always be the door that needs work, the energy (muscles) may need some strengthening. Again, it takes time. Patience will be your best ally in this. Focus on what you want to achieve, and spirit guides will help you with the rest.

CHAPTER EIGHTEEN
Medium Beware

I know we've all heard the slogan "buyer beware." We hear that often due to experiences people have had with fake psychics or scams out there that will take advantage of people looking for help. Clients can usually look up information on the psychic or medium to get referrals from friends and family they trust. Mediums do not have it so easy. As a professional rescue medium or clearer, you must be aware of the challenges you might have to face during your work. There are a great many people out there who will take advantage of you, steal from you, or try to harm you if you aren't careful. We sometimes let our emotions get in the way of logical and rational thinking, but you must remember to keep a level mind when doing this work to stay out of trouble. A few hints that I always recommend to new rescue mediums out in the field:

Never go alone. Now I know this must be a silly statement because why would you ever go somewhere you've never been alone. Trust me, it's surprising how many people do. And why do they? They want to help someone in need. Their healing heart can't stand to have someone wait for help if they can't find someone to go with them. This can be the worst decision you make. Never go anywhere you haven't been before or meet someone new alone for any reason. Security is a big issue in today's world. Pay close attention to your surroundings and always have a phone on you for emergencies. Try to go during the daytime if possible as well, and leave the area if you feel uncomfortable. Spirits do not need to be rescued only at night. Though you may receive more action at night because of the quieter energy, spirits will still come out during the day if you ask them to show themselves. As a general rule, you really shouldn't be doing rescue work alone anyway. You should have a clearer with you when you work to help in the clearing process. I have my clearer work with me not only to work on energy stimulation in the place but to protect my energy while I'm working with spirit. Also, it can take a while to clear residual energy so having help with you is essential.

Try not to work for free when you do a rescue. This is really just a suggestion. Charging a fee is not a requirement and should be handled at your discretion. The reason why I mention this is because it can be one of the biggest problems we have as investigators, mediums, or clearers in this field. Most clients do not feel that this service should be charged for. They say it's a gift, and you should not charge to help spirits go into the light. Actually, you aren't charging the spirit anything; you are charging the client for services rendered. You're taking your time, your money, and your effort to come to someone's assistance if you're doing a residential or business rescue/clearing. The price we spend on clearing tools like crystals, incense, sage, singing bowls, or other tools of the trade can add up over time. I'm not saying to charge a huge fee, but charging enough to cover expenses for gas, clearing tools, and your personal time should be expected. If you do all your work for free, you're essentially paying them to work. Would you ask a talented plumber to fix your sink for free?

Try not to give free readings when you get called to investigate, clear, or rescue. Again, this is at your discretion. There will be people who will try to take advantage of the medium's time when they are at the location and try to get in a free reading when you are working in rescue/clearing mode. Your position at that time is to clear or rescue, not provide a full-blown reading. To be clear, it's your time and your effort, so do what you think is right for you. I will say again, you're giving your services away for free. If you normally charge a fee for your mediumship readings, then you should be charging a fee and list it as a separate service if they want to connect to spirits on the other side for a reading. You might allow this to occur on occasion depending on the situation, but you'll learn over time that when you give an inch, people will take a mile.

Keep on guard when dealing with new clients. Half the clients who call you for help do not have earthbound spirits, negative energy, residual energy, or any sort of supernatural event going on. There are those out there who feed on attention from others. They will demand that they have things going on in their home when they actually don't. You'll also get mentally unstable people who think they are being attacked by demons or aliens, and they need your help. Not all dense and dark energy will be coming from the spirit. Dangerous or unstable conditions in the home can create a feeling of paranormal activity. The best advice I can give is to talk to the client outside with your co-worker for awhile to get a feel for what is going on and what might be going on in the mind of your new client before entering any residence or business. If you get an uneasy feeling, trust it and walk away!

Be careful about angry clients looking to promote their business. Quite often owners of hotels, restaurants, museums, or old historical sites call you in to prove or certify the existence of spirit activity. They do this for monetary gain. If a spirit is detected, they can promote their business as haunted, which draws in a larger crowd in certain areas. During these times, businessowners will ask you not to rescue the spirit or help them into the light. Keeping the spirit earthbound is more profitable for their business. If you should find yourself in this situation, please be very clear that your main purpose is to aid in the rescue of the spirit. The spirit's healing come first, unless the spirit needs to be cleared for safety and security reasons. Promoting businesses isn't our focus and that needs to be stressed. A portion of businessowners will ask you to leave once you explain what you do. Try not to put up a fight or argue your point. The businessowners have the right to do as they wish with their own business. They don't, however, have the right to decide if a spirit should transition or not. That's up to the spirit. If you feel the spirit needs help and is ready to move on, you can complete an indirect rescue for the spirit off-site.

Be aware, there will be times when you do not sense the activity of spirits, only residual energy, and the client can get upset. They may try to degrade you and publicly ridicule you if you do not show proof of a spirit. This is a defensive maneuver to disprove your gifts and try to show that spirits are still at their business site. Try not to take it personally. Not everyone has the same morality as you. Just stay firm with your decision and try not to be manipulated.

Make sure you are allowed to be where you are. Certain places may need permission before you are allowed to investigate. Even if a client calls you into a public place because they feel spirit energy, it's your responsibility to check if you are allowed to be there or not. Do not rely on the word of the client, unless they own the public or private place. Public domains such as shopping centers, parks, cemeteries, schools, or restaurants may also have hours of operation that must be adhered to. Coming onto the premises after business hours can be risky and possibly illegal, so checking all hours of operation will be important.

Check for permits if you need to smudge or leave items behind to do a special clearing. The best example is if you go to someone's house and they have a lot of residual energy in the backyard. You may want to build a small fire to smudge the area. Most cities and towns will require a permit for that. Always check to be safe.

Act like a professional so you don't upset the client. People will expect you to be a figure of authority when they call you in for help. If anyone on your team isn't being professional, you may upset the client and may be told to leave. Unprofessional activity from teams may include damage to property, usage of personal property, or unwanted personal advice. You're serving as a representative of rescue mediums. It gives all of us a bad name if you or anyone on your team acts up.

Do not post anything on social media about your investigation, rescue, or clearing without a written authorization from the client. You can't even imagine the type of trouble you will be in if a client finds out you posted on social media about them and their situation without approval. This is an invasion of privacy. Even if you receive written approval, it's usually best to change names and personal information out of respect. It's up to you and the client. Remember, always cover yourself!

In Conclusion

I want to personally thank all of you for your support and work in rescue mediumship. The field of rescue mediumship has really come a long way throughout the years. I'm so happy with its progression and acceptance in the spiritual communities and look forward to its continual growth. I feel so blessed to be part of such an amazing spiritual and psychic field of mediumship that gives hope and inspiration to so many.

We are just beginning to understand the cycles of death and rebirth, and the world of the earthbound spirit is a big part of that understanding. Knowing that death is a personal experience that changes from one person to the next helps us understand the expansiveness of our spiritual life.

We must also know that with the help of our spiritual loved ones on the other side, we are never alone and must look to them for knowledge and support. We cannot do this work alone, and, therefore, we must build a strong relationship with our spiritual team in order to be successful.

The world of spirit is magnificent, waiting for us to explore and understand so that we continue to evolve as spiritual beings in a physical world. Always look to further your development, no matter how far you've come. There is always more to learn.

The field of rescue mediumship continues to grow and expand so that many others will follow our footsteps to serve a greater purpose. Though I pray that one day rescue mediums will no longer be needed and that all spirits can transition without the assistance and encouragement from us, I know it's not going to happen overnight. As spiritual beings in a physical world, we still have a lot to learn. I'm sure we will get there, one step at a time.

Please feel free to reach out to me with any comments or questions you have regarding your development and work in the field of spirit rescue. You're never alone, and help is always available if you should need it. My hope is that through this book mediums and those who wish to be become mediums are inspired to carry on my work, bringing the light to those who have lost their way. As a rescue medium, there may come a time when you will be the only light in the darkness for a soul in need. With the help of this book, your guides, and your team, you will light the way.

Please visit amymajor.com for more information regarding my books, classes, events, and services.

I wish you the very best. God bless.